MAGICAL HABITS

WRITING MATTERS!   A series edited by Lauren Berlant,

Saidiya Hartman, Erica Rand, and Kathleen Stewart

Magical Habits

MONICA HUERTA

Habits

DUKE UNIVERSITY PRESS
Durham and London 2021

Designed by Aimee C. Harrison
Typeset in Portrait Text and Helvetica Neue
by Copperline Book Services

Library of Congress Cataloging-in-Publication Data
Names: Huerta, Monica, [date] author.
Title: Magical habits / Monica Huerta.
Other titles: Writing matters! (Duke University Press)
Description: Durham : Duke University Press, 2021. | Series: Writing
matters! | Includes bibliographical references.
Identifiers: LCCN 2020044109 (print)
LCCN 2020044110 (ebook)
ISBN 9781478013266 (hardcover)
ISBN 9781478014171 (paperback)
ISBN 9781478021483 (ebook)
Subjects: LCSH: Ethnic restaurants—Illinois—Chicago. | Mexican
American cooking—Social aspects. | Food habits—Social aspects—
United States. | Mexican Americans—Ethnic identity. | Mexican
Americans—Illinois—Chicago. | Cultural pluralism—Illinois—
Chicago. | Decolonization—Study and teaching (Higher) | Feminist
criticism.
Classification: LCC TX715.2.S69 H84 2021 (print) | LCC TX715.2.S69
(ebook) | DDC 647.95773/11—dc23
LC record available at https://lccn.loc.gov/2020044109
LC ebook record available at https://lccn.loc.gov/2020044110

Cover art: Digital reproduction of lithograph of *Vespertilio-homo*
on the moon. Originally printed in the *New York Sun*, on
August 31, 1835. Photograph of Chicago skyline by Jeff Brown.

Publication of this book is supported by Duke University Press's
Scholars of Color First Book Fund.

Para tí.

contents

IN WHAT FOLLOWS, dear reader, you will notice there are times when I use the first-person plural, *we* or *us*. Might I ask for your patience? It is not always obvious whom I mean, and it's for this reason: I don't know.

This book seeks to enact as much as describe. When I use *we*, therefore, I imagine it more as a liturgical than a declarative or prescriptive utterance. It's liturgical in this sense: in church, there were times when the priest's *we* would include me ("Give us this day our daily bread") and times when it would not ("We believe in One God, the Father, the Almighty"). No one quite gave me permission to identify or opt out, but the space was nonetheless available between the altar and me. Therefore, just as I ask for some patience, I also intend this note as an invitation.

I write in anticipation that some who have come to these pages will feel acknowledged. Svetlana Boym writes that "the nostalgic is looking for a spiritual addressee. Encountering silence, [s]he looks for memorable signs, desperately misreading them."[1] I wonder if it's possible to hold that misreadings can take us both into and out of nostalgia, if encountering memorable signs in what reveal themselves, over time, as misreadings can also release us, and if instead of looking for a spiritual addressee, I might be able to sustain—as a practice and a habit and a ritual—the conditional. If I were to have already found one, or many. If not, the fair truth is that that's how many books disappear, even those which studiously, humbly avoid either the first-person plural or an invitation. And so I take this other risk. Alone when I write *we*, but maybe soon with some company.

preface a patron saint

A STATUE OF BENITO JUÁREZ stands in a small, tree-lined plaza beside the Wrigley Building, at the bend between the northern and eastern branches of the Chicago River. His figure is small enough that his metal clothing sits biggish on him. A more compassionate sculptor might have shrunk the coat to make it fit. Under the coat, bow tie, buttoned vest, and overcoat that reaches just below his knees, he hides one hand behind his back and relaxes the other at his side. It's an old-fashioned shape for repose, meant to emphasize, perhaps, that Juárez the Man belonged to a different time. His face wrinkles faintly around marked features and looks over as pedestrians and traffic glide along Michigan Avenue. Yet, even if tucked away, at the bend of a river, in the shadow of a building, Juárez the Statue, our (this book's and my) patron saint, presses very much on the present in a way that could undo us all.

I first found Juárez the Statue while conducting research for my senior thesis. I was surprised to find him there, in part because I hadn't been looking for him. Genuinely interested in an answer, I asked him, What are you doing here? And with both seriousness and a sense of play, he shot back, What are *you* doing here?

It happens that Abraham Lincoln greatly admired Juárez. Their terms as presidents coincided not only in chronology and civil war violence, but in the contours of the conservatisms and liberalisms that fractured their national polities. As president of Mexico, Juárez also contended with international wars, as when the Mexican army fought off a French invasion. For this and other reasons, he was called "the Mexican Lincoln" by some.[2] In turn, it was in part Lincoln's support for Juárez's efforts against the French that gained Lincoln respect from some Latin American leaders—especially as an emblem of a broad sense of "American" possibilities set apart from US imperial designs. The Mexican victory against the French was a particularly surprising one because the Mexican treasury was then still crippled by the imperial land grab that our textbooks refer to as the Mexican-American War (1846–48). (Lincoln, while a congressman, had publicly opposed the war.) Through its invasion and military victory, including a march through Mexico City, the United States seized not only millions of acres, but also the eventual wealth from both the California gold mines and the oil rigs of the Southwest. Yet, drawing these divestments and profits together, one sees again settler colonial nations relying on displacements, dispossession, and violence to build up their coffers.

In the war's aftermath, millions of Mexico's citizens—some of whom thought of themselves as Hispanos with cultural ties to Spain—were given the option of becoming American citizens. Historian Laura Gómez has said that the war "should be understood as the moment in which Mexican Americans first became constituted as a racial group."[3] Whether Mexicans were a distinct race, however, would become its own legal and cultural tangle over time.[4] And that tangle would carry with it an insistence that Yomaira Figueroa-Vásquez has characterized this way: "The insistence on Latinidad as mestizaje, a triumphant and vigorous mixing of 'three races' to produce a unifying ethnicity in which we are 'all mixed'—café con leche, unos más café, otros más leche—holds the same underlying structures of anti-Blackness and anti-Indigeneity as Anglo and U.S. racial hierarchies based on hypodescent."[5]

⇒

On March 21, 1999, Mayor Richard M. Daley, the heir to Chicago's Daley family political machine (the bearers of the most local version of white supremacy of this story), recognized Juárez the Man as both a "Great President of Mexico" and as a "Hero of the Americas."[6] These are the words emblazoned on the plaque that accompanies the statue. But as the first indigenous Mexican president, his particular occupation of that political office bucks against the very claims of the postcolonial, criollo, settler-national sovereignty it rests on. In the United States perhaps even more so, because, of course, the office of the president of Mexico has no jurisdiction in the Chicago built on Ojibwe, Odawa, Potawatomi, Miami, Ho-Chunk, Otoe, Missouria, Iowas, Meskwaki, Menominee, Sauk, Kickapoo, and Illini Confederacy lands. One paradox of Juárez's presidency was that he oversaw a massive eradication of collective indigenous rights, even as he was Zapotec.[7]

But as a symbolic arrivant to Chicago, his indigeneity nonetheless reminds us of the unstable jurisdiction of "Chicago" as a product of ongoing environmental devastation and dispossession, and of the consolidation of contemporary nation states through the same.[8] The statue's ability to stand in as a heroic symbol for all the Americas, while in Chicago, renders his presidency beside the point, his heroism perhaps (and unintentionally) more oriented toward a future that hasn't yet arrived and for which Juárez himself might not have prayed. For reasons that Mayor Daley can't have meant, that Juárez the Man might not have asked, Juárez the Statue nonetheless asks all of us who are not recognizable through relations as indigenous to these lands: What are you doing here? Let's hear the question politically and existentially, in the viscera where those tend to join.

Also unbeknownst (it feels safe to assume) to the board that selected Juárez the Man for recognition with Juárez the Statue beside the Wrigley Building, that building is likewise the product of a series of embedded, contested histories. The William Wrigley Jr. Company accumulated a fortune built from selling chewing gum, as though to really pinpoint how susceptible people are to suggestion: we'll chew just for the sake of it if someone artfully suggests we have the need. The company had its offices in the Wrigley Building until 2012, the same year the city designated the site as a landmark. It was designed by the architectural firm Graham, Anderson, Probst, and White and completed in 1924. The architect most responsible for its design, Charles Beersman, took inspiration from French Renaissance and Spanish revival styles, but specifically had the Giralda Tower of Seville's Cathedral in mind. Originally built as a minaret, the Giralda Tower was a tower for another god. But the building in Chicago looks enough like the cathedral-mosque to remind us that, in the early twentieth century when skyscrapers were first being imagined and built, architects were among those who believed their science might save humanity.

We haven't outgrown the architect's desire, and it's a good thing, when so many registers of catastrophe are undeniably plain, no matter what stories one is using to understand or deny them. But in the institutions and professions that have built up around the social role of aiming to make knowledge (and sometimes aiming at saving humanity with it), the largest rewards accrue to those who make heroic claims, as though anticipating our own statues. The first study of its kind. A discovery. A solution. New insight. This bears immanently on our present. Restitution. Recovery. Some of them are, in their way. In their way. But the heroic posture our professional and institutional structures ask us to perform rubs against the specialization of our trainings, the finitude of our resources, the multiple and ongoing collaborations necessary to actualize any project, the crumbling of political-material investments in education and social infrastructure more broadly. The professional structures that validate treating the enterprises of education like property to be bought and sold—paradigmatically owned—and, whether intellectual or otherwise, the logics of property always already belie any "before property" and those that we might yet summon. In more than one way, property rights are a claim to time as a claim to eternity. The heroic posture, then, is the projection of the property logic—even when the heroic posture announces the limit points built into every kind of knowledge and knowing, even new knowledges and new knowings. And we uphold it, because we have bills, and because it feels good to wear, like a biggish coat.

One could venture that the heroic posture depends on those limit points; that in fact those limit points are the only reason to keep claiming discovery, arrival, uncovering, solving—in order to keep solving and arriving. This is emphatically not, by any stretch, a critique of those limit points. Quite the opposite. I'm more wary of the impulse for claiming or wanting a Totalizing Knowledge than of even these heroic postures. This is, rather, an appreciation of how important it could be, for those relatively few of us whose work is recognized as making knowledge from within a professional enterprise of making knowledge, to appreciate and name our limits just as much as our vantage, our practices, our habits of mind. And so this book takes up the limits of ways of knowing to sing in the growing scholarly band that aspires toward some otherwise, with Ruha Benjamin, with Lauren Berlant, with Stephen Best, with J. Kameron Carter, with Sarah Cervenak, with Ashon Crawley, with Eve Ewing, with Yomaira Figueroa-Vásquez, with Alexis Pauline Gumbs, with Saidiya Hartman, with R. A. Judy, with Tiffany Lethabo King, with Fred Moten, with C. Riley Snorton, with Kathleen Stewart, with Priscilla Wald, with Judith Weisenfeld. I am grateful to write in a time when there are so very many more.

Of specific concern to this book are certain habits of thought to which we've been called in the hopes of both deconstructing racial and settler-colonial capitalism's structural and philosophical life and filling out historical archives shaped through and by these historical violences and imbalances of power. This book performs the question of whether these same critical imperatives—meant to liberate minds and so futures—can be livably lived in, that is, what they yield to and in a life when critical turns of thought are practiced like habits for living. Partly, through their critical practice I propose that constantly exhuming archives looking for versions of certainty can also become suffocating; that living as critique can manifest dizziness, distance, loneliness; that critique can take us far in a thick accounting with the past for the present, in an archaeology for the future, but falters as a mechanism for deciding what kind of choice or change it's time to fight for. As Neetu Khanna asks in *The Visceral Logics of Decolonization*, "How are we to feel new feelings?"[9] If critique can bring us closer to contending with multiple temporalities, our locations amid these, and the feel of the material world that enraptures and incarcerates and murders, this books digs in at the join where someone has to decide what to do, how to stay tender, become honest (by bringing close the intimate project of "being honest with yourself" with the more public one of "education" with the more explicitly political one of having and abiding by allegiances), but also to keep going with room for joy. On most days I would fight you and say this last part is paramount.

In all, *Magical Habits* is an experiment that takes inspiration from, for example, Alexis Pauline Gumbs's poetic trilogy: *Spill: Scenes of Black Feminist Fugitivity*, *M Archive: After the End of the World*, and *Dub: Finding Ceremony*. I aim at a lived-in process in solidarity with an abolitionist praxis, understood, after Ruth Wilson Gilmore, as a consequence of divesting while presencing at once, and of affectively, spiritually, intellectually pressing toward a different political horizon but in such a way as to hold the institutional and structural divestment and reimagining toward which various collectives and coalitions push as also an entry point for reimagining everyday relations outside, especially, carceral logics, which work in important ways with property's logics. As I have understood it (I am still learning) and taking leadership and drawing insights from the many generations of scholars and organizers like Mariame Kaba who have been doing this work, an abolitionist praxis requires, among other things, placing yourself, too, in relation to every manifestation, current, and countercurrent of history, and especially the structures and institutions whose primary outcomes are quickening death and thickening suffering for some. This while, at the same time, actively imagining and implementing the *where* that a pivot toward elsewhere—an elsewhere away from historical repetition—leads. Here, I aim to write the personal differently. In keeping with the spirit of experiment (this book works more like a series of questions rather than a handbook or argument), I also allow for missteps and incompletion on the way to both assuming and inviting that horizon. *If I were already to have found them. If we were already to be a we, you and I.*

Magical Habits aims to find and articulate this unstable edge, between the practices of producing knowledges toward decolonization and the habits of living, sometimes in unfreedom, that some of those modes of thinking can nonetheless beget.[10] This is because, in addition to making knowledge, I and what follows are invested in what it means, and what it takes to stay urgently attentive, but also supple and free, and how to cultivate multiple modes, multiple habits of thought rather than proposing there is one way of knowing, one genre, one discipline, one posture that can save us. That is, I'm invested in insisting that there are no heroes, just us and the habits we might choose to insist on and inch our ways to elsewhere.

What follows owes an obvious debt to a feminist mode of storytelling as criticism, inspired by scholars like Lauren Berlant and Kathleen Stewart, Black feminists from Sojourner Truth to Sylvia Wynter to Saidiya Hartman, and Latina feminists, especially those who find a theoretical origin with Gloria Anzaldúa. As with hybrid texts like *Borderlands/La Frontera*, *The Hundreds*, and *Wayward Lives, Beautiful Experiments*, this one practices omnivorous writing first to honor what each mode yields, to honor each as its own genre and so episteme, any of which needn't claim primacy or universality in a world enmeshed in and reproduced through radical difference and differentiation. I share the aims of these feminist traditions as with those who sought and seek to theorize beyond white-cis-hetero-masculinity's acutely limited vantage, especially about how to imagine and hold and relate to a capacious historicity of settler-colonial racial capitalism, its contradictions unresolved, its afterlives potent and thriving, while at the same time cultivating some other future than the one most probable through a logical (often genocidal) extension of those same afterlives.[11]

At the same time, I also peer out from decades of misunderstandings of the Combahee River Collective's notion of "identity politics"—those willful, those unwilled. Keeanga-Yamahtta Taylor, for one, has done important work to clarify these misunderstandings. The collective wrote, "We believe that the most profound and potentially most radical politics come directly out of our own identity."[12] As someone who grew up privileged in important ways, mostly beige, and ethnically ambiguous looking to some, I had to do a different kind of work to find and make the allegiances through which to articulate a more holistic politics. But there was no other beginning than through my position and positionality, and with disinvesting from the hierarchies that made the same possible, palpable, pleasurable—and without the need for recognition for this, which is also doing the very least.

Most often, inside and outside our classrooms, when a "vantage point" is proposed, the assumption is that a person's biography created it, and that biography, especially its identity markers and foundational structures, can become exemplary of those markers, those structures. And yes, in their way. And no, not entirely or exactly. By now, it's a maxim that any viewpoint is subjective, and also something much more than that because the structures that helped create it are broader, the markers historical. The connection between identity and politics was a practical one, that we learn about the world from where we stand, and if we stand in relation to structures of power whereby the power enforces limitations on our lives, we know more about those structures than those wielding their power.

And alongside the misreadings of the Combahee River Collective the personal need not have a proprietary (and so exclusive) relationship with those broader historical forces on account of their vantage. It can be helpful to parse the lived possibilities for finding a radical politics from the knowledges made available by various positions in relation to power. After all, the claim Anzaldúa makes is not only about the existence of a "new mestiza consciousness" but about that consciousness as a way of knowing. And in proposing it as a way of knowing, she proposes a work of imagination, a process of having been learned, having been practiced, in line, for one, with William James's notion that all knowledge is teleological.

It's first a way of knowing because a structural position produced it. But a way of knowing needn't only be comprehended or even shared exclusively from within that structural position, even if and even as there are key and foundational aspects of felt experience that are shared, shared broadly, and shared through highly specific material and affective pathways. The point nonetheless is that a way of knowing can be learned, even if a life lived from within its production by specific structures might not be able to be entirely, neatly empathized with from another location in relation to those structures.

It (empathy) is an important question, but, just like what's idiosyncratic about these personalized yet structurally produced vantage points, how important empathy needs to be in any moment and in any account is a local, rather than a structural, question. The daily torture of racism, classism, and cis-gendered heteronormative patriarchy can transform our spiritual needs for empathy into seeming as though they should be or might be structurally resolved. Material inequities require structural transformation. But even if it breaks our hearts and keeps us yearning (and for many, we've now moved far beyond the desire for empathy's offerings), no empathy has ever been successfully prescribed, by either structures, saviors, or stories.[13] Examples can be given and described, but need ever to be lived out, imperfectly, and according to the utterly human pace of one by one by one. This is, in part, the structure of empathy: there is no crisp prescription; only the intended receiver gets to decide if it's been given. And who are any who have committed active, ongoing, unrelenting harm to say to any other, This should be good enough for you.

Plainly then, my aim in what follows is neither empathy nor recognition—excursions which, in a certain moment, could be crucial but which are also so often unsuccessful. As critic-authors like Namwali Serpell have explored, there are not only real imaginative limits to empathy's promises and to seeking recognition through words and pictures, but there are also common violences in the midst of both.[14] Even more plainly: on account of my relative material stability and privileged though not harm-free trajectory through racialized matrices, in the pages that follow I do not need either empathy or recognition from you. And whenever I can help it (I cannot always help it), I am not here (in the local sense of this book, and in the broadest sense) to be consumed, enjoyed, or comprehensively comprehended. I have other needs and desires, and in the world we inherited, these are a luxury good I hope to put to good use here.

These are just some of the ways in which what follows departs from the critical tradition of (auto)biomythography that has a root in Audre Lorde's *Zami*, even as the stories here will reverberate against the same. These works, up through memoirs such as Carmen Maria Machado's brilliant *In the Dream House* and Myriam Gurba's resplendent *Mean*, marshal narrative and history toward expanding the grounds of recognizability for a varied authorial *I*. In these pages, *I* serves the accumulation of a questioning practice about our relation to archives, history, and nostalgia. The *I* that travels here gathers and disperses without an interest in culminating, appearing, or restoring archives. There is, then, more in common with Sharon Holland's reading of the biomythographical in novels where *I* is a question or the grounds for questioning.[15] It's with this latter impulse of narration that what follows picks up and drops out of the personal: not toward recognition or historical restitution (though some of that might happen along the way), but toward an experimenting *I* as a dissolving ground from which and toward which emerge the historical, the familial, and the fictional as another set of questions. Put another way, I try to write inside/outside the propertied logics that tend to authorize personal writing. Juárez the Statue and I looking askance at one another, asking: What are you doing here?

It's fitting, then, that our patron saint offers his promise of another future from beside—and not inside—his temple, looking away from it but never able to leave. He's on the threshold of the conditions of his own possibility, capable of seeing just past it, after it but also not searching for another imperium. One of the challenges this book proposes is about that kind of intellectual and emotional openness as a habit of thinking and feeling: Is it sustainable—and how?—to keep being open to finding your and your thinking's limits? More: that his temple's style betrays layers of intertwined imperial and colonial histories renders both emblematic of how quickly a local story becomes global if it's allowed to bleed, and how the ends of those stories can nonetheless stay open: What are you doing here? As a kind of answer, our patron saint of questions reaches backward and forward in time, unsettles his own presumptions of authority, and disregards any neat boundaries between history, useful accidents of interpretation, and whatever happens next. Let's decide he's the patron saint of this book by being the patron saint of all of that, of an inclination, of an opening, of insisting, a capacity for loving beyond knowing for certain and becoming safe (worthy) of that kind of love in return.

The writing in this book, then, follows Juárez the Statue's symbolic and affective lead. It arises from the particulars I know best, of growing up in Chicago's Mexican restaurants; extraparticular histories that reach out into global flows are one, and a more familiar, answer to the question of what we are doing here. But those particulars are also the vantage point from which my writing seeks out the unlivable limits of some of our critical habits for history. To those ends, I take on several modes of writing. Each approaches history and critical historical practices from its own generic and intellectual strengths. The numbered pieces work most like criticism in both an associative and personal mode, closest in spirit to what C. Nadia Seremetakis has called "micrological ethnographic sites" that "trace, translate and analyze cultural phenomena and practices as performative dynamics of and in everyday life" even as "they are cross cut by recurrent themes."[16] These portions of *Magical Habits*, then, are written as the kind of ethnography—of producing and encountering thinking as a critic about and with history—from within the "dynamics of and in everyday life" and often from the vantage of childhood and youth, sites of so much open and undisciplined theorizing, though not often taken in as such by scholarly cultures and conventions. The dated pieces are fictionalized echoes that an archival dig could miss but that are nonetheless pieced together from inherited family oral histories. Some names have been changed to protect privacy, others have not. These two—the numbered and the dated—are in an ongoing dialogue about the relationship between self, history, and storytelling habits as self- and world-making. The single fairy tale playfully extends the philosophical ramifications of this dialogue by dramatizing perhaps the most popular mariachi ballad in Latin America, sung ritualistically in any relation to masculinity and with aspirations toward being "El Rey," despite, so the lyrics go, not having a throne, a queen, nor anyone who understands you.

Throughout, I've included bits of documents and images that gesture toward the kind of archive that informs still another mode of writing in which I work here, a sketching of a cultural history of Mexican restaurants in Chicago. I first took on that project as a college senior, just as I met Juárez the Statue. I include it here, edited for clarity, to signal the writing practice most familiar to scholars. I also include it to make plain once again—by way of contrast with the other writing—the liveliness its conventions miss. As a wonderful reader of this manuscript helpfully put it, genre here acts as "a holding environment" for all the questions I ask.

My writing as a scholar-in-training is also a provocation to consider what it can do for us and our intellectual cultures not to partake in the fiction of our own scholarly progression as along a trajectory of linear time. Much as we might deconstruct both those notions—progress, time—for scholars, it's nonetheless possible to imagine that somehow our aging begets something better, more, more heroic. I suppose this choice on my part is a kind of professional risk. I would write this cultural history differently were I writing it now. But the hope is that the humility inherent in the gesture of making scholarship into its own intimate archive might also be a productive one. Even if only to insist as much by translating what else happened beyond any book's margins. And yet, how would our postures of "understanding" shift away from the heroic if we thought of the process not as one marked by accumulation (a propertied affair), but as one of continually divesting previous habits, and then seeking to divest again? What writer hasn't suggested it? I write the book as the book writes me.

Offering these modes of writing as part of an intertwined critical project, I loosen the strict, generic bind of each while nonetheless holding up their intellectual promise.[17] The hope is to help cultivate a more capacious livability in our thinking that honors irresolution's affective strain, that is, the work of living decently (ethically) and rigorously in a world built such that choosing both can be excruciating, while at the same time proposing the humility of wandering eagerly and attentively toward our needs (another name for our limits) as toward one another as toward the horizon abolitionists articulate. It's also a call to be responsible for becoming a safe haven. The hero's journey, after all, can be paralyzing in its loneliness, and the rewards of that journey—even if victory were possible, as in conquering one single archive once and for all—more likely to be empty of joy. Accolades are nice but rarely snuggle or dance with us. Why not keep bending our writing and our thinking toward opening up the possibilities for ever more rewarding practices and habits, where the reward is the chance at more chances of making ever more freedom into lived, material realities? The rewards might be about divesting, giving up the gods hidden over by professionalism's marriage to the way capital, for one, has structured the shape of our fields of inquiry.[18] It can be a revolution: to pray differently, that is, to take on scholarly rituals that lead to elsewhere—an elsewhere that's unknown in any definitive sense, but must, nonetheless, exist. That is, if as knowledge-makers possibilities are primarily what we desire to be opening?

Because, finally and urgently, I want us to make all and any forms of knowledge while and as we honor the sacks of tender, feeling flesh we drag to computers, to libraries, and back home after long days, overwrought with and underloved from history; honor the students who trust us with their potential; honor the beloveds waiting patiently or impatiently for us to finish that thought; honor us all without re-creating habits that cordon off one portion from another, that ask us to sacrifice ways of knowing in order to feel like a hero in a diorama we've created from a shoebox. For these reasons, my critical wanderings stubbornly refuse to choose one mode, one habit, one genre, one kind of knowledge and knowing. In practicing and making habits from the multiple, in writing from and as the relentless limits of the multiple (rather than another heroic, Whitmanesque version of multiplicity), I reach beyond the powerful, bewitching idea of one, not to conquer but to offer, and to find a way to genuflect toward our patron saint as a mode of dignity rather than abasement. If we sacrifice the singular hero and the need for the same, there's a chance (however fragile, however sincere, however hopeful, however simple) we'll gain one another. That, too, is what I am doing here.

I. the synthesis problem

Together these precious family articles constitute what one might call the magical legacy of the people; they are conceived as such by their owner, by the initiate he gives them to, by the ancestor who endowed the clan with them, and by the founding hero of the clan to whom the spirits gave them. —MARCEL MAUSS, *The Gift: Forms and Functions of Exchange in Archaic Societies*

THERE WERE GIFTS. A platinum Cartier watch with gold rivets for my twelfth birthday. It sat for years in the medicine cabinet, beside the Visine and Midol. An antique ruby and diamond bracelet from Tiffany's I wore twice, both times for him to see it. A gold teddy bear charm with tiny diamonds mounted on the bow around its collar. I liked how smooth, rounded gold tasted and felt on my tongue; I bit the bear until it had a dent in its back. A car at fifteen: a black Land Rover with cream leather seats. Four months later, I tore it through a wooden fence, and flipped into two backyards, narrowly missing a sunbathing mom lounging by her pool. My friend and I had to climb out through the passenger-side window, inhaling burned rubber, and mud, and grass, beyond our ability to tell them apart. A tie-dyed Beanie Baby bear, sent by FedEx from Guadalajara for my seventeenth birthday. A rose gold Cartier watch with pink diamonds around the face for my twenty-fifth birthday. Before I left New York the first time, someone I knew (he'd washed the dishes clean of his fingerprints and taken out the garbage) broke into my apartment and stole what hadn't by then been destroyed, misplaced, or given away, even the fancy luggage I used to carry it all each time I moved.

The last one, for my thirtieth birthday, a brokerage account in my name that was "lost" during their divorce. The questions I had were about timing: Why now? Where has it been? Did you know to look for it, or did it find you? And did you try to cash it before sending me a printout of the balance? Somewhere in the shuffle of places and time, in the shifting ground of needs and desires, I gave up the need to know certain things certainly; there are entire lifetimes that could pass (that have passed) digging in—especially—the most stable ground. Even if some questions can acquire a faint smell and linger, can make quiet thick like soup, I accepted the brokerage account with a simple thank-you note. Better to pray for swift winds, and the wisdom to know the difference between which and which and for when.

He wore belts with large silver and gold buckles engraved with his name, a horse, or a horseshoe. Sometimes the figures were outlined with rhinestones. Parece un ranchero, my mother sometimes said in a way that let me know I never wanted to be that before I knew exactly what she meant, before I could place the word in a place, let alone a style, and definitely not in a story or in time, and before I knew that words can have a perspective and hold antagonism and ambition at the same time. After the Ultra SlimFast years, he wore belts with the designer etched and hidden into the backside of the leather. It was the desire to believe in an exclusively triumphant world, like a fairy tale where you end up sophisticated and just snap your fingers, click your heels, poof, zap, presto change-o, and abracadabra. At one point or another, you might learn what it means to have taste and that taste might be somehow important, and then later that the importance is only ever paid for with someone else's blood. And here you are anyway, tangled in what's earnest and tender about needing small comforts, loud coups.

It was his grumpiness that reminded her of "the one with Archie Bunker"— that's what she called her favorite show, Where his wife is singing at the piano, she'd say, and with his pretty daughter. What does he call the son-in-law? ¡Ja ja ja! ¡Sí! Meathead. Cara de torta! Face of sandwich/hoagie, Sandwich-/Hoagie-Face, is the right translation even though it's not the correct one, Cabeza de carne, Carne cabeza. How much left over from not having the heart to tell her the difference, what horizons of parentage hold the possibility that it's you who watches your parents either grow up or refuse to?

He doesn't know what he is saying half the time. His brain works faster than his mouth. Someone needs to follow him around with a tape recorder. He would lose his head if it weren't attached to his neck, she said. Sarcasm can hold pity (another kind of allegation), but at least pity can breed a kind of love, and if they tend to you as you lay dying, what difference does it make; or, it does, but what's surprising is how small the difference can look at that end.

No matter the belt, no matter the shape of his belly, his pants drooped, and made an inward slope. He is the only one in my family with a butt so flat that the fabric of his pants meets the back of his thighs in a muffled bunch exactly where mine are full, not loud but operatic and straining. On Sunday mornings he ate breakfast in white briefs and a white V-neck T-shirt, then climbed back up the stairs, backside toward the hallway to the breakfast room where we all sat. I smiled while my mom and sister laughed at it, proving again how easy it is to be buoyed into a slightly brighter morning by the promise of someone else's embarrassment.[1]

There are floor-to-ceiling mirrors in their bathroom where there should be walls. They remind me how cold the floor is on my feet in the morning. This is a *master* bath. It matters if a house has one but I couldn't say why, and then an old habit asks who decided—and when—that a house needed a bath to be the master, and did this bathroom have control over the other ones, and exactly what did that control mean? What words keep a word company matters. The name for that game is context.

After showering, after drying, after pulling clothing over and onto his body, he bathed in cologne: one kind, then another, and another; sometimes a fourth, sometimes on a Sunday. It was exciting to watch him spray, sprinkle, spritz, and dab around his neck, his stomach, his chest, down under his belt, and back up into his scalp. He could be the Mexican Pig-Pen or a Latinx Roadrunner, but slower and with cologne clouds floating around his face instead of dust circling his feet. The plastic buffer at the bottom of the door dragged over the floor when he left, followed by the doorknob's brassy kiss, then the lazy rumble of the garage door opening.

In his cartoon show, whom would he be chasing and who would be running away? Would there be giant molcajetes instead of anvils, Chespirito instead of Wile E. Coyote? If moving between languages can be tricky, does translating pictures work? In Mexico, Plaza Sésamo decided Big Bird–yellow would become first Serapio- and then Abelardo Montoya–green. Then again, invention is messy; especially if you're translating at the same time, there will be some splotches, some left over.[2]

Although: invention can also mean there is actually nothing new except believing, that believing is the trick of people who call themselves alchemists (and academics and entrepreneurs), that invention promises a way outside of time, of making time into a home you grow too big for, to which you wave goodbye only to build a new one, if only to keep reminding yourself. Invention is a strange, loving tradition, one you might get good at if you knew love is not beautiful, symmetrical, with smooth edges, is not perfectly framed, paced, or even anything like form and has much more in common with uncertainty than with romance. It's a lot to risk, with hardly any edge to hold on to.

The priest had a bald spot at the back of his head, where a neck fold met a scalp fold to keep warm. She was eighteen on November 19, 1974, when her bridesmaids wore emerald-green silk dresses with lace trim along the edges of their tulip sleeves, with silver-blue eye shadow on their eyelids all the way to the corners and deep into the folds where their eyes opened. Her teeth were uneven behind deep red lipstick. In the very few pictures I see, their faces all have a silver sheen, from the makeup or from the flash? For a long time, I thought skin shone different in the seventies, the way that in the 80s the whole world coordinated orange and beige and brown and corduroy. I don't know how often or whether they look back at the years since and what they see, or how soon blue eye shadow and green dresses seemed far enough away to have been like a different lifetime. This is how to look askance at your own biography, following the horizons until those are all that's left.[3] It's a lot to risk, with hardly any edge to hold on to.

He took me to see Michael Jordan play, even when he wore the number forty-five. I asked for pop and popcorn after the game had already started so that he had to leave and not see the first shot Jordan made. When he lumbered back down the stairs—our seats were just a few rows above the court, one other gift—I wondered, with twelve-year-old pleasure, if he knew what he'd missed.

MAGICAL HABITS

Casually and cruelly, I told him Jordan scored. Yeah, I know, everyone was going nuts out there, he answered. I resented his enthusiasm. There were so many gifts. I decided not to be bought.

But I do become devoted to certain players as artists, to basketball as comprised of various poetics, not just Jordan's jumpman, Iverson's crossover, Starks's headbutt, Miller's flail, Curry's arcs, Butler's drives, Antetokounmpo's Euro step, Durant's fadeaway. A gift—like a life—can exceed itself and become, instead, a persistent question of whether there's a debt and to whom.

Not long after his father was killed in a factory accident, when my sister was barely a year old, he used his US passport (he was born in Chicago but moved back to Guadalajara when he was twelve) to move back to Chicago. They followed later. Just before contracting a coyote at The Border, she got the phone call that their citizenship papers had come through. They wouldn't have to be "illegal"; bureaucratic whims had decided they could be American instead. At least, that's the way I know the story. Her first acts of citizenship in Chicago were to get braces and turn twenty. She learned to type at her first job as an assistant (the word then was *secretary*). She learned English just well enough by learning how to type quickly. She wore bright red lipstick then, in the silver-sheen photographs, as now, when she works at a nonprofit in Chicago, helping newly arrived migrants find and finance homes. Ever the displaced—uncomfortable, itinerant—who can immediately connect needing a home to another form of waiting for society to redefine its sense of justice.

Migration stories begin with coordinates on a map and a scene change, with a degree of disorientation in time and space and the protagonist on her way from there to here. What would the cinematic be without migrants and migration? The here (my here) is an embattled and forgetful hemisphere, created through and enmeshed in global drifts, flows, and floods. She is excited, expectant, nervous, anxious. She has a bundle of belongings, some photographs of the loved ones she'll miss but who also sometimes misunderstand her, and she awaits whatever versions of the unexpected. Some hardships will be on their way, and a transformation. No matter what, if she is coming to America, America is bound to be the real winner, either through gaining a loyal new daughter or in proving too mighty to be conquered.

My here is an embattled and forgetful hemisphere that connects to the other embattled and forgetful hemisphere. And in both, people are dancing.

I'm descended from centuries of restless migrants, some of them murderers (far enough back, to be sure, and you'll find some in any family tree), some of them adventurers and vagrants, some of them caught up in global capital flows into and away from Mexico in ways that left them hungry, some of them holding tender aspirations, some incarcerated for taking up and taking possession of the oldest form of freedom, the oldest form of survival: to leave one place in search of another. Some of them priests and saints.

But this is also not a historical romance, where, as a reader, you have a marriage to look forward to after inevitable separations, where what I want to offer you is a glimpse into a way of living that might not be familiar to you, as if I were a tour guide and you were on vacation. If this is a romance at all, it is the kind about imperfect stories (sometimes they are just wrong) that might help float you from one place to another, not arriving, but passing through a forgetful hemisphere attached to another forgetful hemisphere by water and atmosphere.

And it's more precise than to say they were married: they owned restaurants together. It was our family joke, not knowing how much more traditional, more historical that made their marriage, the business arrangement structuring the possibilities for love. The restaurants were why I was born in the suburbs of Chicago, and they were also why we drove Downtown every week. I preferred the nighttime drive, when the city was quieter, when she yelled less often at the traffic—¡Mira nomas este imbécil! ¡Me llerve el pecho!—through tense teeth. Her voice made me nervous, it felt like the whole world might break, or maybe just her skin would burst open. She flashed her teeth like she could tear it off. It was years before I thought to translate what it meant to have a boiling chest and realized I never realized the meaning—although in another way, of course I did.

One wrinkle in the conceit of criticism is that language often hits in waves, over stretches of time, finding us as though for the first time years afterward. Each critical act can only be provisional, each argument a suggestion at best. It could carve out, not disinterest, but a habit of disinvesting in the power through which arguments are made to seem final, as though we might stop time—or want to.

At night, I barely identified the skyline as buildings. The lights inside became free-floating patterns of squares, of rectangles, or nineteenth-century compositions of color music, from when circuits of northern Atlantic peoples who became the people who believed they were white believed they were also evolving into better perceptions of color, and wrote music with color in the hopes of encouraging sight to evolve (for white people).[4] So much of knowledge became that way through the many guises force can take. One set of work to peel away the edges to make room. Another to insist there's already space and fill it up with every sense of color.

With the shapes lights made against the darkened sky, I imagined hopping about on them: some higher, some lower, some like a rectangle, some in the shape of a diamond. I didn't like looking, after turning onto Randolph from Lake Shore Drive, when I could tell there were people inside the buildings— so intrusive to pass my eyes over someone else's furniture. This was a problem and the reason for many lawsuits in the late nineteenth and early twentieth centuries. It happened that when elevated rail lines were built in cities like Chicago that were growing farther into the sky, looking out the window of your apartment now meant meeting strangers' eyes on you.[5] It was unnerving then, and if you ask the subjects of photographer Arne Svenson's *The Neighbors*, it's still unnerving. We'd like to be looked at exactly up until the moment we would not like to be looked at, and it matters who is at the other end of the sight line, and it matters how we've come to know what we look like, and it matters, it can matter, what exactly is the mood, and will you hurt me if I ask you to stop? Just some questions embedded in a frame. Just one way to begin to remake the world.

A simple phrase from José Limón's *American Encounters: Greater Mexico, the United States, and the Erotics of Culture*, about the history that Mexican food in the United States might tell us, led me to my parents' archives. They did not call them archives, but I was a History and Literature major in college, so I did. Using those archives and others', I wrote a senior thesis about Mexican restaurants in Chicago after taking summer classes at UCLA in the Chicana/o Studies department. There was and is no such department at Harvard.

The thesis read back into the history of Chicago's mainstream white newspapers for how white food critics talked about encountering Mexican food from the early to the late twentieth century for an audience that was presumed to be white.[6] I conducted interviews and used oral histories from several Mexican restaurant owners in Chicago to dig into what changed over time when Mexican food was deemed "authentic" by anyone except Mexicans. I tried to parse and process and name. I tried to make mine what had been their livelihood (and mine). I tried to reconcile new vocabularies with theirs. I wouldn't have been able to say that.[7]

The first Mexicans we know of settled in Chicago in the early twentieth century, displaced by the social unrest of the Mexican Revolution (1910–21).[8] More than a million people left Mexico during the Revolution, and while most settled in the American Southwest, there were also those who traveled farther north.[9] Like other diasporas, the Mexican communities of Chicago experienced successive migrations over time.[10] Also like other diasporas, the history of Mexicans in Chicago is inextricable from shifts in the perceived needs of "labor markets," as though they were impersonal forces. For example, railroad companies recruited 206 of the Mexicans displaced by the revolution to Chicago, and these (mostly) men established the first permanent Mexican neighborhood in Chicago on either side of Ninety-Fifth Street, between Brandon and Yates Avenues. Those blocks bordered an Irish migrant neighborhood on one side and a settlement of African Americans who had fled the Jim Crow South on the other.[11] As was the case with other migrant groups, factory owners often used some of these Mexican men as strikebreakers during the steel factory strikes in 1919 and strikes at meatpacking plants two years later. These are the kinds of episodes that helped create the specific, local histories of animosity among Chicago's racialized groups.

Like Chinese Americans in the late nineteenth century, Mexican Americans were subjected to a series of massive deportations in the 1930s by the Immigration and Naturalization Service (INS).[12] The deportations were a racist reaction to the precarity experienced by white Americans during the Great Depression. Nationally, over "200,000 such aliens (mostly Mexican) were deported between 1930 and 1940, in addition to the several hundred thousand more (the exact number is unknown) who were forcibly 'repatriated' during the same decade."[13] At the time, 14,645 Mexican Americans lived in the city of Chicago, with another 3,579 residing in the suburbs.[14] During the 1930s, the INS deported half of Chicago's Mexican population; as happens in other mass deportations, some of the deportees were American citizens.[15]

Deportations both affected those who were deported to Mexico and left a profound imprint on the Mexican community in Chicago. Underlying those deportations were assumptions about the innate foreignness of Mexicans in Chicago. At the same time, this continued an American tradition of politically dispensable and racialized labor forces. These experiences of precarity influenced how people of Mexican ancestry felt about a country that did not hesitate to send them away in light of perceived political economic needs and made imaginable and convenient by political economic expediency.

As early as 1942, due to labor shortages during World War II, the federal government once again shifted its policy in order to import Mexican workers. The Mexican Labor Program transported over fifteen thousand Mexican citizens between 1943 and 1945 to the United States. In Chicago, these new migrants found homes in New City, Back of the Yards, and the now mostly Mexican communities of Pilsen and "Little Village."[16] Under the program, agreed to by Mexico's federal government,

> Mexican workers were to be afforded numerous protections with respect to housing, transportation, food, medical needs, and wage rates. . . . The program was extended by subsequent enactment until 1947. For the growers the bracero program proved to be a "bonanza." Braceros were limited exclusively to agricultural work. . . . When the agreement ended December 31, 1947, the program was continued informally and was unregulated until 1951. In that year, under the guise of another war-related labor shortage, the bracero was once again formalized by P.L. 78. This program continued to function until it was unilaterally terminated by the United States on December 21, 1964.[17]

There is more work to be done in understanding how deportations of Mexicans, the bracero program, the use of Mexicans as strikebreakers, and subsequent unionizing among Mexicans and Mexican Americans created the precise contours of Mexican Chicago. At the same time, what we have not known about these local histories has contributed to a mythologizing of the Mexican and Mexican American experience in the United States as existing only in terms of labor—labor the United States needs or doesn't need, dignity that can or cannot be wrought from laboring, depending on what are perceived as macroeconomic needs.

In Chicago, as part of a new energy around consolidating a Mexican American community, a "Mexican Social Center opened in 1945 [and] was dedicated to the memory of Manuel Perez, who had won the Congressional Medal of Honor during World War II," just one of many Mexican American veterans who shared the destiny of Black veterans upon returning to the United States.[18] In addition to the Mexican Social Center, organizations such as the Mexican American Civic Committee, founded in Chicago in 1943, and the Mexican American Council, founded in 1950, demonstrate that there was a need to build separate spaces focused around socializing with other people of Mexican descent.[19] At the same time, other political battles, like the four-year struggle for the Benito Juárez High School in the 1970s, suggest that, even though political leaders dedicated to them were scarce, Mexicans and Mexican Americans nonetheless found a way to wield power in Chicago. In this episode, Mexican community members wanted to prevent their children from being bussed out of the district and successfully demonstrated outside the Board of Education's meeting.[20]

In the late 1960s, though there had been Mexicans in Chicago for at least two generations, there were also newer migrants who were able to speak of their country of origin with the authority of lived experience. For example, the culturally hybrid invocations of the Chicano Movement at once glorified Mexican culture through deploying Aztec symbols, at the same time that they self-consciously rooted the movement in the context of the United States, through slogans such as "Brown Power" and "Brown is beautiful" echoing African Americans' reinventions through affirmations of their history. Chicanos in the late 1960s and 1970s imagined a fictive land of Aztlán, what they called the American Southwest, as their homeland. Aztlán itself was emblematic of Chicanos' identity as constant cultural negotiation, not quite "Mexican," not quite "American," at the same time that it oversimplified and homogenized indigeneity as it had been and was being lived out in Mexico as throughout the hemisphere.

In the process cruelly termed "urban renewal," Chicago's historic Mexican neighborhoods had to relocate southward to the areas now known as Pilsen and La Villita. These still serve as cultural centers and receiving grounds for newly emigrated Mexicans, even though most of Chicago's Mexicans no longer live there.[21]

Where some academics once attempted to fit Mexican political integration into the turn-of-the-twentieth-century "white ethnic" model of assimilation, others recognize that Mexicans have often chosen to negotiate between allegiances to two modern nations.[22] Michael Jones-Correa explains Latinos' low naturalization rates in terms of the cost of naturalization, divorced from issues of discriminatory practices inherent in the process.[23] He refers to the "politics of the in-between," where certain types of political mobilization take place and have origins in the negotiation between cultures and polities. This "politics of the in-between" is similar to the complicated process of cultural negotiation, reproduction, and performance that occurs in the Mexican diaspora in Chicago.[24]

At the same time that a narrative and experience of fragmentation persists, the early foundation of social organizations, the Chicano Power movement, and other types of organizing also demonstrate shared grounds within the Mexican diaspora in Chicago. That is to say, the Mexican communities in Chicago have been produced through cultural transformation just as much as they are an engine for the same. Constructing a "homeland" in the myth of Aztlán is a way of claiming the terms of exile at the same time that the myth expresses a complicated relation to Mexicanness in the first place. Yet, projecting the

MAGICAL HABITS

idea of Mexico in Chicago through the use of Aztec symbols creates a largely fictional and nonaspirational return to Mexico just as it creates new emotional pathways in Chicago for what those symbols mean and, finally, vexes their own relations as arrivants, like Juárez the Statue, on unceded indigenous land.

Some days she tended bar under rows of glasses hanging upside down. I let myself believe they hung in midair on their own. There are still times I would rather be enchanted by what I don't understand. Then in school I learned about magnets and thought *magnets in the bases of the glasses* held them in place upside down. The day I was tall enough, I reached up to grab one and found slots in the ceiling where the stems fit, and so one form of magic left me. Here is what no one tells you: if you were to solve all the mysteries, it is the same as being alone.

When she smiled at customers and when she listened to what they had to say, I couldn't tell if or when she meant it. What they didn't know that I knew is that her jaw might be tense behind a smile.

Other days she was in the kitchen, wearing heels that got stuck in rubber mats. From walking into and out of the kitchen to find her, I know the different sounds of different kinds of shoes sticking to rubber mats at the end of a day (hers, mine, yours): sometimes a squish, sometimes a squeak, sometimes a click. Like the aggressive, pointed kisses of someone who would smirk with the next breath. I know how dirty a restaurant can get. I know it doesn't mean the food is bad or that anyone in the kitchen is unclean or uncareful. I know what grease smells like when it's old; it's how I came to believe air has a memory and ghosts might be real. I know the floor can be sticky and greasy and it doesn't mean it's not washed every night. I know how gray the water is when it leaks out onto the back alley, after the floors and mats are hosed off. I know how to forget the splatters on the cook's apron.

It's obvious, from this vantage point, that Taylorism and Fordism missed the point, and so what of spending years upending what's already, on face value, a farce?

There are other things that seem like a secret: that hairnets leave an indentation on foreheads when you take them off, red and pink grooves worn in with time and tightness. It was all I'd ever seen, so I thought black hair belonged under a hairnet. (There's no way to disavow what you've never owned as your own, no matter the price in pride.) I had dark hair too, but I took for granted I would never wear one, the kind of knowing that doesn't feel like I ever learned it. The kind of knowing that happens in an accumulation of gifts if they stay just themselves and the pleasure they were bought to buy, if they don't become a question: what are you doing here?

Something like condescension crept in thicker than a work ethic (just one way I laid waste to your racial logics and found a way to wield them), and too late to avoid regret, it occurred to me that someone might have imagined more than once that I belonged in a hairnet instead of wherever else I was. And at that exact moment—a sum total of the moments before regret—I had more in common with the one imagining me in one, incapable of any holistic imagination of justice that includes prioritizing well-being and life in such a way where a hairnet becomes some other kind of sign than one for shrinking possibilities around any life. Just then, and in each instance thereafter, what could either trinkets or belt buckles prove?

Allegiances are not born with blood itself, no matter the comfort, no matter the terror the idea inspires, no matter the number of times it's asserted that affiliations are a natural occurrence, appearing in the east and setting in the west like the sun, looped together with history. But they might begin to be earned by asking forgiveness, first of oneself for taking so long to choose, which, depending on the urgency and the need in the moment, can be any time at all.

AUGUST 2003 *Cambridge, Massachusett homelands*
REVISED NOVEMBER 2018 *Philadelphia, Lenni-Lenape homelands*

MAGICAL HABITS

c. 1982

Author's personal collection

CARNES

Steaks

CARNE ASADA **5.95**
Strip of skirt steak grilled to perfection;
served with fries.

CARNE A LA TAMPIQUENA **6.95**
Same as above with guacamole and one
enchilada with your choice of filler;
served with fries.

CARNE A LA MEXICANA **5.95**
Chopped tenderloin simmered with butter,
tomato, onion, green pepper and garlic.

BISTEC RANCHERO **5.95**
Steak cooked in our own special
Ranchero sauce.

Above served with Rice, Beans, Lettuce.
Tomato and Corn or Flour Tortillas

Salud, Dinero, Amor.....
y Tiempo para Gozarlo

BURRITOS **2.50**
Large flour tortilla rolled with beans and
your choice of beans, beef or chicken filler)
(Steak, pork, avocado or Mexican sausage
—$.50 extra)

BURRITO DELUXE **3.50**
Same as above with lettuce, tomato,
cheese, sour cream, avocado and your
own special Ranchero sauce. Your choice
of beans, beef or chicken filler.
(Steak, pork, avocado or Mexican sausage
—$.50 extra)

BURRITO SUIZO **3.50**
Same as *Burrito* with sour cream,
topped with our own special Ranchero
sauce and baked with melted Chihuahua
cheese on top. Your choice of beans,
beef or chicken filler.
(Steak, pork, avocado or Mexican sausage
—$.50 extra)

BURRITO SUIZO DELUXE **4.50**

ORDENES EXTRAS
Side Orders:

Spanish Rice	1.50
Refried Beans	1.50
Refried Beans with Melted Cheese	1.95
French Fries	.75
Sour Cream	1.00
Tortilla Chips	1.00

Salvador's Restaurantes Mexicanos menu cover

c. 1983

Author's personal collection

"The Burrito Dream," from Salvador's Restaurantes Mexicanos menu

c. 1983

Author's personal collection

The Burrito Dream...

Once upon a time, a poor little Mexican boy in Chicago had a dream of cooking the biggest burrito in the world. After many years of dreaming, he went back to Guadalajara in Mexico to the "University" of San Juan, De Dios Market, and started to learn how he could fulfill his dream. He worked very hard, day and night cooking and cooking until he got the recipe right.

While in Guadalajara he thought it would be easier if he had a partner, but he couldn't afford it, so he got married to a poor little Mexican girl from Guadalajara. Now he was ready. He loaded everything on his burro and walked for many days and nights with his burro, his Lupe, and his recipe book.

When they got to the Rio Grande all three suddenly learned how to swim.

Hiding from immigration and doging cars and trailers from the expressway, all three made it to Chicago and started to fulfill his dream.

Visit our 1st Location at 700 N. Dearborn, Chicago, our second at 134 N. Ridgeland Avenue in Oak Park, and all our other locations in Chicago and throughout the world!

A poor little Mexican boy.
SALVADOR

SEE YOU FOR YOUR NEXT FIESTA.

GRACIAS

Salvador's Restaurantes Mexicanos rejected logo treatment

c. 1989

Author's personal collection

Salvador's Express rejected logo treatments

c. 1990
Author's personal collection

Salvador's Restaurantes Mexicanos logo treatment

c. 1995
Author's personal collection

We would be honored with Your presence to preview the most authentic Mexican Restaurant in Chicago.

For fifteen years Salvador's has been serving the best Mexican food in Chicago, now come and see his dream come true of design, décor, atmosphere and the real Mexican food that with his Margarita made him famous.

January 9, 1991
5:00 p.m. – 7:00 p.m.

Hors d'oeuvres and Open Bar
Entertainment: Mariachi Azteca

Salvador's
Route 83 & 75th Street
Willowbrook, Illinois 60521

Please R.S.V.P. to (708) 850-7974 or (708) 325-4666

June 1993
Author's personal collection

VOICE 1 [Over a soft rock band.]
There's a different restaurant in Chicago that has combined a number of different restaurants into one, where you can dine on the finest Mexican food and also rock out on their dance floor. The one name you'll need to know for all your needs is Salvador's.

VOICE 2 [Mariachi music.]
Salvador's, you say, why that's just a Mexican restaurant on Wabash Avenue between Lake and Randolph.

VOICE 1 [Soft rock band.]
No amigo, Salvador's is more than just a Mexican restaurant. Salvador's has mucho rápido lunches for the businessperson on the go. Also Salvador's has live bands, rock bands, dance bands in their own upstairs nightclub. Friday through Saturday start the weekend right at Salvador's. Just a Mexican restaurant? Hardly, amigo. Salvador's happy hour is from 4 'til 7, Monday through Friday . . . and all sports including Cubs games can be seen on their giant TV. If you thought Salvador's was just a Mexican restaurant, you've got . . .

[Mariachi music.]

another thing coming . . .

c. 1995
Author's personal collection

Salvador's is proud to offer the most authentic gourmet Mexican cuisine in the Chicagoland area. Its mouth-watering delicacies include a variety of "homemade" mole based dishes, such as poblano, verse, pipian, ranchero & chipotle plus an extensive salsa variety. In our grill you will savour fresh seafood, catch of the day, grilled, baked or broiled, "Acapulco style" fresh sopes, "charro" beans and home-made tortillas & tamales.

You can enjoy real Mexican appetizers (tapas) anytime of the day.

In our Pub & Cantina is Fiesta time all the time, no Siesta for us, Live Mexican music, mariachis, guitars, tequila, "Mucho ambiente." We dare you to be brave and bold, when you order our World Famous "Salvador's" original "killer" margarita, a mere 48 oz. Jug of Joy!!! We've got the lushest Piñas Coladas, mai-tais, tequila sunrise, sangria, and the best Kahlúa drinks, this side of the Rio Grande.

More fun at a "Salvador's" in Chicago, Lombard, Willowbrook, Oak Park, Illinois, and Boca Raton, Florida.

Experience and enjoy the "whole enchilada" with your host and amigo Salvador.

Mi casa es su casa.

SALVADOR HUERTA *[Handwritten]*

2. fabulation

It can be dangerous to investigate what our lives depend on, to recognize that freedom requires a species-scale betrayal of our founding mythologies. —ALEXIS PAULINE GUMBS, *Dub: Finding Ceremony*

THE MEXICAN ARMY was hunting Catholics. Or Mexican Catholics were tracking the roots of anticlerical governmental reforms. My great-grandfather, Salvador Huerta Gutiérrez, was arrested either as he was on his way home or on his way to work at his garage. The version someone told me was that he had been holding mass in secret, and someone had told someone else who wasn't supposed to find out. The army was also looking for his brothers, Eduardo and José, both priests. After being questioned and tortured, Salvador was shot by the firing squad against a wall of the Panteón Mezquitán, and so the body did not have to travel far.

This was not the first time that the Catholic Church and the Mexican state had had rocky relations, and not the first time that members of the church had been persecuted. In some ways, the tension between the Mexican government—itself working to reimagine a postcolonial, postrevolutionary, modern state—and Catholicism had been written in the stars.[1] If it was the stars that dictated the shape of Spanish colonialism. And if it was the stars that ushered in the Bourbon reforms of the eighteenth century, which expulsed Jesuits, alienated the lower clergy, and so laid the groundwork for independence by aligning the cause of independence with the clergy decades before Padre Miguel Hidalgo y Costilla let out el grito de la independencia from a church tower. Months later he would be beheaded.

Salvador Huerta Gutiérrez and Adelina Jiménez, married April 1907. Originally printed in Alatorre Huerta, *Salvador Huerta Gutiérrez*, 24.

Besides what we think we are doing as we're learning and writing and teaching, and besides how much more like an anatomist it might feel to sidestep stars, what is the effect of the difference between discerning a constellation and attributing contingency? We have to decide which caused which, which is the independent variable and which is the dependent variable. Yes, but there can also be no accounts to count.

In a universe of dark energy and dark matter, nothing is only just still outside the desires to make them so. In the universe we're floating in right now, the kind of difference between independent and dependent variables as we imagine them evaporates. But on the human scale, we also experience those differences even as they evaporate.[2]

He was born during the Porfiriato in Magdalena, Jalisco, in 1880—just barely a Pisces—and baptized the next year. His birth certificate states that his parents, Isaac Huerta Tomé and Florencia Gutiérrez Olivo, whose marriage in 1866 was the very first recorded in the first book of the Registro Civil de Magdalena, which itself had been instituted by Benito Juárez, were "mexicano/a no indígena."[3] Those were the choices and a choice had to be made—if it was not overdetermined or prescribed.

One of his daughters, María Guadalupe Huerta Jiménez, remembered his eyes this way: "Tenía los ojos grandes de color café verdoso, con ojeras que los hacían verse mas profundos. Hablaba con los ojos; aunque no abriera la boca, te lo decía todo con la mirada."[4] Magdalena is a ways from Guadalajara, to the northwest, where his family would eventually move, and where both sides of my family eventually arrived and multiplied. His two older brothers enrolled in the seminary there, and his brother Ezequiel, who was known for his singing voice, worked as an organist in the church. My uncle Antonio, named for my grandfather, inherited the talent, and was able to have a bit of a career as a singer. He even, I'm told, went on tour with Maná. With Antonio I couldn't tell the difference between his well-worn habits of care, in which he lavished praise on everyone through elaborate floral arrangements of affection, and those that were directed solely at me. And really, it was lovely enough to be under his spell it hardly mattered. Just after turning fifty-four, a heart attack killed him.

Family lore has it that Salvador was a serious child, who minded his chores and took pride in being disciplined. But his discipline was not oriented toward academics, and after completing the equivalent of high school, he began working, first in the mines in Zacatecas, then on railroad cars in Aguascalientes, and finally as an auto mechanic for either a German man or a German company. There are conflicting stories. It was while working for the railroad that he met and fell in love with Adelina Jiménez. Given that Salvador was a railroad worker and because he was ten years her senior, both families were opposed to the relationship and, later, to the marriage. Nevertheless, after a courtship that is said to have involved communication through a three-centimeter hole in a window, with Salvador on his knees so that his mouth was at the height of the hole and so that he would not have to shout, they married. It's said that the wedding photo included here is not from their wedding day. For whatever reason, there had not been time on the actual wedding day to take a photo. It was on another day entirely that Salvador had told Adelina to put on her wedding dress and veil to go to the photographer's studio.

Together, they had ten children: Salvador (1908), María (1909), Guadalupe (1911), Gabriel (1913), Dolores (1914), Isabel (1917), Antonio (1919; my grandfather), Francisco (1921), José Luis (1924), and Isaac (1924). You could say my pursuit of stubbornness began here. Not because of bloodlines, but with the ancestral flourish of defying parental forbidding through having, instead of none and nothing, ten children.[5] After he, his wife, and their oldest children moved back to Guadalajara from Aguascalientes, Salvador opened an auto repair shop, where he employed, at most, eight people.

In the way it's often said of martyrs, it's said of him that while he was working in mines, on the railroad, and on cars, Salvador had several close brushes with death. Once, a boulder fell on and killed someone who had just replaced him at work; another time the cable on a mine's elevator broke. That accident killed almost everyone but him and a few others. It's also said that he liked opera music and going to the movies, and that he was an attentive father and husband. I'd like to say there are sweet stories passed down through my grandfather, his son, that I inherited. There aren't. These are the bits that I've gathered in the way that my job trained me to gather them, through publications.

So I don't know what subtle or unsubtle forms and feelings of piety led him to join the Adoración Nocturna Mexicana in 1921, which was recognized by Pope Pius X in 1913 and had been granted, among other things, the power of plenary indulgences. Although the secularizing 1917 constitution had already been passed, he couldn't have foreseen the strict versions of enforcement that would be imagined shortly thereafter. Part of his pledge as an active member of the Adoración was to offer Jesús a night "de amor y sacrificio" every month as penance for the sins of the world, not just for his own. In addition, as part of his devotional practice, he led his family in praying the rosary each night.

In his contribution to the ongoing conflict over how much power the Catholic Church should have, and whether and how it should be separate from the Mexican state, President Plutarco Elías Calles outlawed wearing religious clothing in public (for clerics, monks, nuns) as well as religious education. These and other restrictions spurred violent skirmishes, so that his eldest son, Salvador, and two of his nephews, Manuel and José de Jesús, left Guadalajara to join those fighting in what was to become known as the Cristero Rebellion, La Cristiada.[6] The fighting started in the summer of 1926.

On April 1, 1927, his older brother Ezequiel visited his house so that they could mourn the day's executions of several Cristero leaders, including Anacleto González Flores, who had been a member of the Catholic Association of Young Mexicans, and later the National League for the Defense of Religious Freedom. Flores, along with two brothers, Jorge and Ramón Vargas González, were brutally tortured and ultimately killed when they would not give up any information. It was after Salvador and Ezequiel had gone to pay their respects that they were both apprehended, questioned, tortured, and themselves executed in either the darkness or the dawn between the daytimes of April 2 and April 3. They'd refused to give General Jesús M. Ferreira the whereabouts of either their brothers or the Bishop Orozco y Jiménez. The story is that, just beforehand, Salvador opened his shirt and held a lit candle to his chest so that the firing squad could more easily aim at his heart.

I sat next to his grandson, my dad, in a Guadalajara soccer stadium and watched people slowly filter in. The day was for consecrating the kind of faith and conviction that, when pitted against state power, ends in death and leaves relics. My aunt and some other family members had worked for years to make it happen. They petitioned the bishops, the archbishop. Martyrs, in order to be martyrs, need to be recognized; their symbolism only works through memory and the stories that sustain it. For this ceremony the Pope chose twelve Cristeros for recognition through beatification, my great-grandfather among them. My grandfather Antonio would have been around eight years old when his father held a candle to his bare chest.

There's something in the passionate veneration of martyrs that echoes by way of inversion how easily most lives end soundlessly. These "untexted" deaths might ask us to respond; the dirtiest secrets and deepest historical

Huerta (middle) and either coworkers at the railroad in Aguascalientes or
employees at his auto shop in Guadalajara. Originally printed in Alatorre Huerta,
Salvador Huerta Gutiérrez, 31.

hauntings hide in what is left unspoken, and power lies in the ability to un-
earth and make known. History so often meets the present as an unmarked
grave. One way to mark them could be to reclaim their silence as sacred, to
reclaim what's unmarked as the site of (un)holy battles lost and won. Not a
legalistic right to be forgotten, as in Europe, not a bureaucracy to ensure the
right box is checked on your license: organ donor, check; forgotten, check;

or, not forgotten, check.[7] Maybe to begin, a candle lit. A pause. A stadium full of pauses.

Some had taken buses from nearby towns and cities to honor their holy dead, to honor the holiness they were thankful to have inherited, to honor the new meaning the ceremony could give mass, and lunch, and children. Ushers handed out streamers and pamphlets emblazoned "¡Viva Cristo Rey!" as you walked in the gates that usually held in soccer rituals. The chant "¡Viva Cristo Rey!" (Long live Christ the King!) was the call that the Cristeros had used when fighting, and with one another. It's the last words many of the martyrs are said to have spoken.

"I don't know too many details. He didn't tell long stories. But when he was a kid, the Mexican army took his father away and shot him. He didn't really talk about it when we were kids, but I could tell it was hard, whenever anyone in the family brought him up. He got very serious, not sad, but very serious, like he was talking about the most important thing he would ever talk about. My sister thinks all of that, his father's death, was why he was how he was. Strict. Principled. Inflexible. Unforgiving. If there was love in there, I only knew after.

"The Mexican government didn't want people to be going to church, to mass, then. They closed all the churches. They thought if people listened to what the priest said, they wouldn't pay attention to the government. That's right, one king! Same as now, it's all about who is in power, and power is about controlling information. It's not just government or even guns, whoever controls information controls people, but it started then, not with TV or the Internet or spies, but newspapers and telegrams and the little grandmothers had secret places they would go to pray. And before that, priests! And monks!

"The government outlawed mass, and told the priests to leave the country. The priests had gotten too powerful, had too much land and too much money, and were competing with the government for the people's attention. But you know people, or, at least, I know Mexicans. If they wanted mass, especially the abuelitas, they were going to have their mass. You can't tell an abuelita she can't: she'll fight you! ¡Ja! And she'll win! So people started holding services in their houses. And my grandfather did that. He was very religious, and believed in God and Jesus and the Holy Spirit, the whole thing. He thought it was his duty as a Mexican to believe in the church.

MAGICAL HABITS

"I only heard the story one time. I was listening from the other room and he didn't know I was there. One of his only friends was over, and it was late at night. I woke up in time to hear him tell it.

"They took him without explaining why. With his brothers and sisters, he watched the men with guns take him away. That was the last time any of them saw him, including my grandmother. They wouldn't allow visits in the jail. No one was there when he was shot. But it mattered to my father that he had been that kind of man.

"He named me after his father. I try not to think about it. ¡Ja!"

In 2007 in Tlaquepaque, construction began on the enormous Santuario de los Mártires de Cristo Rey in honor of the beatified Cristeros. Its sanctuary is meant to seat thousands of congregants and to serve as both a residence for retired, elderly, and ailing Mexican bishops and as a medical hospital for the underserved.[8] Over ten thousand people attended the first services in 2015.[9]

We each had fathers who died when we were young: my father, his father, me. The man who was my father is technically alive; I could guess that he is in Guadalajara, but in the last few years I had an account, Facebook let me know he was trying to sell his house there, so who's to say, even if there are people I could ask. The one who died I mourned more like a story I overheard and only later became attached to, faintly, like a memory already vanishing, the contours already evaporating between dependent and independent variables. Lineages have their limits. It can be easier to claim them if you can see them and see them as the entirety of space that makes room for you and other worlds. Seeking after a single thread, it is easy to get caught in the crosshairs of time and urgency; it isn't always a matter of fault or fealty. A world of grace if history needn't be our map especially when we can map it: not in order to avoid its worst lessons, but to find enough room to fulfill them.

And yet, from any way of looking, there can only be more, shimmering or at least vibrating nearby. Some of it impinges on us (or inside, as pressure from the liver, the spleen, just under the left shoulder), some of it we have to choose if it's chosen at all. The wisdom that can be a portal, a portal that opens only with a leap. There's so much else worth feeling, I've tried to make some room, and an altar for the rest.[10] An altar can honor a deity. An altar can offer rest.

My great-grandfather's relic lives there: an ornate silver cross, with the Virgen de Guadalupe painted on an enamel circle above the small glass oval encasing a scrap of his bloody shirt. That is, it was a cross until being shuffled about in boxes during several of my moves. Two of the arms have broken off. I've laid them just below its base, in case throwing them out is bad luck. I don't really know how relics work, or whether they bear a relationship to luck, but this is the kind of thing where I play it safe. It is there with a small Buddha figure a buddy gave me, a large metal disk with Ganesh carved into it from my friend's mother, some palo santo from a friend, a plastic glow-in-the-dark Virgin Mary my grandmother gave me when I was too young to say no but still young enough to make a fuss about taking it, a vase I try and fail to keep filled with fresh flowers, a wooden box for writing down and setting intentions, some smooth stones from different beaches and from Kabuki Springs and Spa in San Francisco, and some important photographs. My scattered relics are blessed in the sense that they have small, potent meanings, quieter, for the most part, than my great-grandfather's cross. There's no Catholic prayers or battle cry I recite, just a kind of surrender where I stay stubborn enough to recognize myself, little more than a pulse across every dimension.

DECEMBER 2016 *Princeton, Lenni-Lenape homelands*

1988

"MUY, PERO *MUY* BIENVENIDA a todos que nos estén escuchando en este, otro precioso día en downtown Chicago. Están escuchando a 'Sábados con Sabooorrrr' en Salvadoooorrrr's! Yo soy Salvador Huerta y aquí tengo el placer de estar otra vez—¡Ja ja ja!—¡Sí! Otra chingada vez con mi muy, muy, muy, *muy* buen amigo el señor Don Carlitos Rojas en Salvador's en Randolph Street en downtown Chi-ca-gooo!

"Gracias a Dios que no se cansa de mí, don Carlitos! Todos los sábados! ¡Ja ja ja! Aquí, a ver, qué come?

"Aquí lo traigo comiendo el burrito más grande de su vida, casi ni puede respirar el cabrón! Y a ver, qué más? Unas garnachitas con pollo asado, un caldototooote de pollo. No puede ni hablar, pero su carita me cuenta que es el mejor guacamole que ha comido en su vida! Fí-ja-te no más! Ay, Don Carlitos! Claro que sí, Don Carlitos, mi Carlitos, para servirle mi broder. Es un gran, gran placer estar con usted. Que gusto me da verlo, servirle una rica comidita, y más, estar aquí con todos ustedes este sábado, que como todos los sábados es un sábado con sabooorrrr!!

"Si nunca nos han visitado aquí en Salvador's . . . pero qué chingados esperan?! ¡Ja ja ja! Vénganse en chinga a Restaurantes Mexicanos Salvador's en Randolph, cómanse un menudito después de la peda que se echaron ayer o no? Pues sí porque sí, verdá! Aquí estamos y así estamos para serviles! ¡Ja ja ja!

"O mira, si les queda retiradito, no hay problema! Segurito que tenemos un Salvador's cerquita de donde estén. A ver, si están por el norte, nos encuentran en Oak Park en la North Ridgeland Avenue. El número, a ver, dónde esta mi vieja? Gorda! Cuál es la dirección. ¡Ja ja ja! Cuidado Gorda, que no se te tire eso! ¡Ja ja ja! A ver aquí me lo trae mi gorda. Ciento treinta y cuatrrrrrro North Ridgeland Avenue, allí estamos para servirle con mucho gusto. Pregunten por mi cuñado, el los atenderá con muchísimo, muchísimo gusto. Tómense una margarita, en ese ahorita tenemos una promoción que si se pueden tomar una margarita grande y comerse un burrito grande, se llevan a casa una sorpresa! Sí Carlitos, una surprise! Surprise, surprise! ¡Ja ja ja! Así es que vayan!—vayan y no se lo pierdan!

"No, fíjate Carlitos, que el Salvador's de Villa Park y el de Irving Park ya no esta. Así es, pero acabamos de abrir otro Crazy Burrito que les ofrece a todos nuestro patrocedores comidita para llevar entre la Wells y la State. Así es, mi broder, así es, antes estaba en la Wells, pero ahora se encuentra allí por la State.

"Aquí? Ay, Don Carlitos, ya ni me acuerdo! Creo que tengo yo aquí casi veinte años. Tu dices aquí en este Salvador's? Ay, sí, no, sí, es muy diferente, mi broder. ¡Ja ja! En este tenemos seis añitos nada nadita más. En el de Oak Park, siete. Así es mi Carlitos.

"Uy, Carlitos, ya casi ni me acuerdo! Nos han visitado tan-tantisisísimos. A ver, Angélica María, Cantinflas, David Reynoso, José José. . . . Ehm, claro que todos conocen a Mike Singletary, sí él también. ¡Ja ja ja! ¡Así es! Le gustaban las margaritas, pero no las jumbo, las jumbo jumbo! Casi casi puedes darte un remojón dentro de ellas! ¡Ja ja ja!

"¡Sí! Como no, mi compadre, hasta la Oprah ha venido a los Restaurantes Salvador's! Pero ella nos visita en el de la Clark. Sí, en la Clark y la Erie. ¡Chips y guacamole, le encanta el guacamole! ¡Pero no tanto como a mí! ¡Ni madres, ni me llega!"

3. disciplines and disciples

It was about this time that I conceiv'd the bold and arduous Project of arriving at moral Perfection. I wish'd to live without committing any Fault at any time; I would conquer all that either Natural Inclination, Custom, or Company might lead me into. . . . But I soon found I had undertaken a Task of more Difficulty than I had imagined: While my Care was employ'd in guarding against one Fault, I was often surpris'd by another. Habit took the Advantage of Inattention. Inclination was sometimes too strong for Reason.—BENJAMIN FRANKLIN, *The Autobiography of Benjamin Franklin*

THINK, IF YOU WILL, of *disciplines* as a kind of magic some people know how to practice until it's as though they always knew, either the hunkering down or the cordoning off of parts of the world and the interplay of meaning that gave them to us in order to stake claim to different registers of facts apart from their stories. Property rights are not just objects of critique, after all; they are also one structure of our affective relations to the felt intimacy of thoughts.[1] It's not sexy, among other things, but it's the only way to make rationality seem sexy, and bind the gesture up with the working of power as a sleight of hand. Property rights were (are) also a mechanism of legitimized dispossession.[2] These are some of the erotics of writing books through one another, of being enmeshed in the ritual dispossessions that make our books and egos possible. One docile and lonely bunny appears.

The way Middle English could be a mother tongue is not as itself but as a loosening of our relation to language. There is no way to read or say it perfectly. There were ships, and diseases, and armies, and theft, and rape, and destruction, the regalia of conquest. When a language is only idiosyncratically inscribed, daily, lived-in sounds largely escape our forms of accounting, and so the pathways of violence too. (It can be a relief.) So it is now (as then) a language kept alive by choice and custom and power; you have to keep choosing to know and pass it on even as you are inventing it. Along dis-remembered pathways of inscription, most of us didn't lose our mother so much as have her become impossible to figure.[3] But even in a cosmic void, even in the voids that exist where we'd like to find a record, there's not nothing, and we're here. The possibilities are not unconstrained, but we could hear them differently. It doesn't have to be this one, or only this one. The way that every and each grito bifurcates, cracks, crumbles, but needs to begin if it's to begin and give us a way to know gusto from the inside out.

It so happens that if you look up the word *discipline*, *The Oxford English Dictionary* sends you to Chaucer's "The Canon's Yeoman's Tale" as an early (scripted) occurrence of the word. The yeoman (generally a farmer, but he could also be a royal servant) tells readers a story about his master, a canon. In the second part, he tells of a canon (not his master) who liked to trick people into thinking he was teaching them alchemy. In the story, the canon sells his secrets to a priest (a believer by profession). While showing how the process works, the canon covers the priest's eyes with powder "by accident" and places a ball of wax with silver fillings into the coals so it seems like silver magically appeared while the priest struggled to clean his eyes. Then, when the priest isn't looking, the canon brings a silver tray out from under his sleeve, on which he's been heating quicksilver and a powder that the yeoman narrator does not name.[4]

The word *discipline* materializes in the story just as the canon "demonstrates" a second time, so that the priest can later re-create "this disciplyne and this crafty science." The priest begs him to set a price and they agree on forty pounds for the fake knowledge. The canon swears the priest to secrecy: if people found out, the canon says, he'd be killed.

Readers know what's next. The priest tries to re-create the crafty science. It doesn't work.

If you read and believe the yeoman, *discipline* can just be the sleight of hand that makes you think something has been created, that you have been transformed into someone who now knows, when it was just a sneeze. Or—and this is every storyteller's favorite trick—the story is the sleight of hand. The yeoman never says what the powder was that made the priest sneeze. Maybe that's the magic, and the story hides it from us to make *us* believe in the storyteller. Reading—the transubstantiation of language into images, made material, then received, perceived, and interpreted—summons apparitions although there is just a book, just some open, orderly shapes across a page, some order we make from open, orderly shapes, some open making. Sorcery. The storyteller: more powerful than alchemy, farmwork, or gods.

The story of the priest ends, and the yeoman turns his attention to Plato and his disciples, which confused me the first time I read it. What is Plato doing here? A disciple asks Plato what Magnasia is. Plato replies, elusively, that it is water made of four elements. Chaucer's Christian Plato gives Christ as the reason for his elusiveness: it is God who chooses to whom to reveal truth, and Plato can't decide for God whom should know. Chaucer pokes fun at trusting disciples tricked (in the first telling) into believing knowledge exists where no knowledge actually exists, and at those who believe in divine revelation where no one owes anyone an account. If you "know," God decided to tell you. If you don't know, God has dissed and dismissed you. The duty was to listen, and it's a disciple's own fault if what they hear is quiet. If you were honest about hearing only quiet, you might also be forever lost. How to listen for which trick history has pulled on you? And how to decide which discipline, or whether disciplines are worth learning on their own if it means also becoming a disciple? No way to decide except, as they say in football, you have to run at the blitz.

The word *familiar* gets tricky even when what's ordinary inspires it. In English it's something comfortable and safe, but the process that made it so is invisible. One says *familiar* when they can't remember when it wasn't. And if I make myself remember, it becomes unfamiliar again—like a puppet that shows and hides its strings, depending on the light. But hearing the word in Spanish, it's more explicitly where blood came from to become part of my atmosphere, another way of describing moving through space toward someone I've always been recognizing. English forgets blood and keeps the secret that time passed. Or did it stop entirely, or never start? When something is familiar in English, it's difficult to parse what's uncanny from what's home even when I no longer live there; the language over-learned Freud. In English it means what is being called familiar has no hope of being made new except by losing its name. Where, in Spanish, *familiar* doesn't get cold: it sparks a birth each time. The more I say the word, the more I think that thinking in English has fooled me into being more forgetful than nostalgic; just when I might need them, there's no source and no imprints. Maybe it's not a language in which to remember after all, if remembering can only mean what I want is to be Sherlock Holmes and turn mysteries into puzzles only I can solve, hoping to distract the world with a sneeze.[5]

⟶

I wanted to go home from the restaurants, inevitably, sooner than my mom could leave. For hours, I sat at a table like a customer who did not come in for dinner. In good moods, I felt important. I did small things others would not have done. I took out my book and read it. I walked up to the bar and served my own drink from the soda gun. I went into the kitchen to grab more chips, to ask for more food, to visit, to watch, to look for my mom, sometimes just because I could. I rested my head on the table to let everyone know how bored I was. I ate all the mints in the basket. In bad moods, I hoped customers could tell they were inconveniencing me by keeping the restaurant open. Being forced to behave in public is an excellent way to learn passive aggression. So is scholarship.

¿Quieres que Lola te haga algo de comer? Quesadillas. I liked the cold sour cream sliding against the greasy cheese that seeped out from the corners. How quesadillas bunched in Saran wrap smelled after an hour packed in a Styrofoam container is how I started to avoid sweating and leftovers at the same time. For no reason except that my face turned red, I became convinced I smelled like that after sweating. I spent my teenage years tracing the reason all the way back to quesadillas sizzling on a stove, which became confused in memory with the damp faces of many cooks, with impatience, with dropping many tiny restaurant mints into my mouth to dissolve, with throwing a tantrum by getting even quieter, by taking back all the lines from my face.

Kitchens to me are grease and steam, and anger, irritation. I disliked guacamole because it was green. I threw away old food with the pleasure of slaying dragons. I grew impulsive and impatient that some rituals might be purely symbolic. Sweat and grease, stoves and faces: repetition and time can build any kind of association until all that's clear is a tangle of ominous feeling. But where's the magic in memory that compels belief, and then which trick sends us in search of an exorcism?

⟶

When I saw him the last time (*When was that?* is not a rhetorical question; I honestly don't know), his hair was platinum and I missed the black curls. What's to miss if we aren't already unmoored and drifting in time? He left the mustache in Chicago. Anything—even a mustache—can be a reminder, especially when someone insists, the way he did, there was nothing worth remembering.

🐦 ....

Born in Chicago and raised in Guadalajara from the age of twelve, Salvador Huerta made his first migration to Chicago in 1976. He was twenty-three. From 1976 to 1997, he owned Salvador's Restaurantes Mexicanos, and like so many restaurant owners, he spoke of the restaurants he opened in Chicago and its suburbs as "authentic." Yet, even the self-presentation of his restaurants raises questions about what then counted as authentically Mexican in Chicago in the 1980s and 1990s.

Far from unique in the lexicon of Mexican restaurants, one glossy plastic menu from Salvador's Restaurantes Mexicanos uses an image of the Alamo to allude both to the borderlands between Mexico and the United States, and a shared moment of Mexican and American history. But the Alamo is merely background for a portrait of Huerta and Guadalupe, his wife. The original photographic portrait was taken at an entertainment center in Bolingbrook, a Chicago suburb, in 1979. Their costumes, worn in a clumsily fashioned "saloon," were meant to evoke the Old West, yet another mythic site of Americanity's constitutive imperialism.[6] But superimposed on the Alamo, with oversized cartridges of ammunition crossing his chest, and a large sombrero looming its shadow over a thickly mustached face, Huerta is meant to resemble Emiliano Zapata rather than an American frontiersman, although it is not clear if it is the mustache or the hat that has been primarily tasked with making the distinction. His then wife Guadalupe Castellanos's "western dress" appears in this context like that of a criolla, whose offspring the Mexican Revolution (that Zapata helped lead) sought to depose from land possession and power.

Through these visual references to the borderlands of hacendados and revolutionaries, the image secures Mexicanness in a preindustrial past, but unintentionally foregrounds the tension between those seen by the law as landowners and those who would claim land by another set of rights. At the same time, the domestic portrait replicates the ways in which family histories authenticate the food being served in restaurants, even as neither Huerta nor Castellanos have direct connections to the Alamo, Texas, Zapata, or any aspect of those specific borderland histories called upon by the image in order to work its magic of recognition. This fictionalized intimacy cloaked in a fictionalized history serves a commercial function; together they create what appears as Mexicanness.

The menu offers an additional text as another blended moment of history and fiction. Inscribed on the inside cover of the same menu is a vignette titled "The Burrito Dream," about a "poor little Mexican boy in Chicago [who] had a dream of cooking the biggest burrito in the world."[7] At first, the boy's dreaming of burritos locates Mexicanness in him despite designating the boy as in Chicago, of Chicago. But over the course of the story, the burrito itself becomes the emblem of Mexicanness. The boy's dreaming leads him to the "University" of San Juan de Dios Market in Guadalajara. Mercado de San Juan de Dios is, in fact, where Huerta operated a stand selling leather goods that his cousin would obtain from a nearby town.

In what is by now a familiar script, the story goes on, "He worked very hard, day and night cooking and cooking until he got the recipe right."[8] For one, this story effaces Huerta's education in "gourmet Mexican" cooking classes in Pilsen to establish authentic Mexicanness in Guadalajara. But more importantly, Chicago acts as the goal and setting for fulfilling the boy's dream even as Chicago's importance in the story shifts from being the place of the boy's dreams to a place of fear and suspicion.

It does so by offering an account of migration that limns Mexicanness with criminality, but also offers a mild critique of the criminalization of migrants. After "load[ing] everything on his burro and walk[ing] for many days and nights with his burro, [and] his [wife] Lupe," the story tells us, they all cross the border. "When they got to the Rio Grande all three suddenly learned how to swim."[9] The fact that Huerta and Castellanos are American citizens off the pages of the menu, of course, contradicts this border-crossing narrative as well as the imagery of "hiding from immigration and dodging cars and trailers from the expressway."[10] At the same time, the story plays into narratives of criminalization of undocumented people, while also implicitly critiquing the same criminalization. Such a depiction of Chicago as a tenuous home complicates the claims of belonging that Huerta, in other spaces, nonetheless espouses. The Burrito Dream did not belong in Mexico; it was born in Chicago. But the portrayal of Chicago as a place both of fear and success is nonetheless an articulation of a way to belong in a place, uncomfortable as that belonging might be. Tellingly, the story's use of a fictitious border crossing is part of its claim to authenticity, and in line with an American tradition of making money from stereotypes.

In the story, Chicago is a place of distrust and alarm as well as of dreams, but it is depicted by a black-and-white drawing of the skyline along a serene Lake Michigan. This architectural vision of Chicago serves as the background for the burrito options in the center section of the menu. Lake Michigan takes up most of the space, as though the couple had crossed it and not the Rio Grande.[11] Here there are no INS cars and no police. Instead, two cartoons again depict Huerta in Mexican revolutionary garb. In the foreground, he sits atop a sagging, sweaty donkey. With another upturned sombrero and smiling under a long, thick, black mustache, he holds a steaming burrito in both hands. A second drawing of Huerta and Castellanos at an open flame shows the couple cooking. Castellanos clutches what seems to be a taco in her hand. She is drawn again wearing the costume meant to evoke a criolla. The sense of Mexicanness here comes in the form of other caricatures, transplanted out of history and onto the Chicago skyline, as though Chicago animates and proliferates these caricatures, a visual lexicon in sleek lines of buildings against the rounded, purposefully clumsy lexicon of caricature. But the figures are undeniably at home as part of the market of value (in multiple senses) that makes the buildings possible.

Huerta chose these images to translate the intimacy of the familial into the saleable. Here, caricature is a solution for the friction of the personal, even as it participates in a visual and historical process of producing and signifying racial differences through stereotypes.

In the restaurants, Huerta said he hoped to cater "to all the segments of the Chicago community as opposed to most of the authentic restaurants who only catered to Mexican customers."[12] His chain, including several fast food locations at different points in time, firmly embraced the commercialization of Mexican food in the late twentieth century. He admits that there was some negotiation at work in presenting Mexicanness to non-Mexican clients. This admission of creating Mexican food is in tension with his own avowed sense of belonging strictly to Mexico even as he was born and raised largely in Chicago.

In contrast to others who share his migration pattern, Huerta rejects any idea of cultural negotiation and chooses to assert a "purely" Mexican identity: "I consider myself 100 percent Mexican. I have always considered myself Mexican, even if I was born in Chicago."[13] He acknowledges that his birth in Chicago might raise doubts about his Mexicanness, but in spite of the ambiguity his American passport might suggest, he explains that he "chose being Mexican because that is what I feel, I never had any doubts."[14] He chose to be Mexican, although he uses the unclear language of "feeling" Mexican. You could ask: What do nationalities feel like?

Around 1987, the financial success of the restaurants inspired an altered version of the logo, which was in use until 1998. In this version, the photograph of Huerta and his wife was transformed, yet again, into a more integrated image.[15] The background was no longer the Alamo, but rather a nondescript adobe structure with two small arched windows. The architecture still located Mexicanness in an amorphous sense of Spanish settler colonial borderlands, but it looked more like a home than a historical landmark. This version of Mexicanness had nothing to do with Chicago: in fact, in this later menu there is no mention of Chicago, and the story "The Burrito Dream," like the Alamo, has also disappeared. Huerta's clothing in the image, however, continues to identify Mexicanness as historical and possibly criminal, that is, as part of a history that is no longer "here," and part of a threat that is ever imminent. Curiously, as the image became more "inauthentic" to itself, that is, more removed from the original photograph of Huerta and Castellanos in the "Old West," it became more integrated into a seamless vision of history—and, by extension, more profitable.[16]

⸻

Part of the staying power of stories like the American Dream is precisely that it is appealing to cast yourself as a hero. It is comforting and affirming to believe that no one worked harder than you, that the success that finds you is the success that you deserve, and that deservingness is an objective category of personal worth. But it can just as likely be the case that the work was hard, that the effort was relentless, and that (any form of) "success" did not arrive. These comfortable stories—no matter who tells them—mute the unease of paying too close attention to widespread, unearned, undeserved suffering, to the hard work of most, done without the infrastructures for dignity.

⸻

The scar on my right hand was under the third knuckle, with rings like an old tree just like his. It started me down this way and had me there for years, the exact number of which I won't count. His scar was from a stove at the restaurant. My hand got caught under a skateboard's red plastic wheel as it was spinning down my cousin's driveway in a Chicago suburb called Justice; it left a tiny splash of blood. I never figured out how it got so far under the wheel when all I was doing was sitting, riding the board and stopping just short of the street. When I lived in California, the rings somehow disappeared into the surrounding skin. If the light hits it right, a faint wrinkle shows up and surprises me, then vanishes again. Not every scar is a mark.

In any city I'm in, when it's taco time, the smell of tortilla chip grease can find me like I'm breathing in a wave's crest and its undertow at the same time.

MAGICAL HABITS

It's old spirits living in that smell, grown brighter and with sweet promises, all the sweeter because they're overripe. But that is not history creeping in with the flood. It's not memory, either (history's fount and echo). In the wave is a series of gestures, like choreography found again, choreography never learned, misplaced, or invented, choreography attuned to some other uninvented time signature.

At some point, we might have to let it go. The bunny, the hold, the sense that anyone—especially any discipline—owns every trick, that life bends only this way and for some. We'll have to let it go or else give up, finally, that other soft idea, with its brittle, forced, violent comfort: that we're innocent of centuries of cutting out other tongues.

APRIL 2013 *Brooklyn, Munsee-Lenape homelands*
REVISED APRIL 2019 *Philadelphia, Lenni-Lenape homelands*

4. aphorism as a promise

Useless to look for another face for them, or to suspect a different greatness in them; they are no longer anything but that which was meant to crush them—neither more nor less.—MICHEL FOUCAULT, "The Life of Infamous Men"

APHORISM GETS PAIRED either with the realm of opinion or of folksy wisdom. It's more traditionally identified with figures like Ben Franklin (Early to bed, early to rise), maybe even your third-grade teacher (A job worth doing is worth doing well), or any elder (Más sabe el diablo por viejo que por diablo; lo que cuenta no es el modelo sino las millas recorridas; dime con quién andas y te diré quién eres). When connected to the idea of "wisdom" or "folk knowledge," an aphorism performs a kind of distillation and crystallization. This aphoristic mode shuts thought, discussion, possibility, down. It entreats, insists, demarcates.

But another tradition of aphorism opens thought up and out. This is that of Emerson (The years teach us much which the days never know) or Nietzsche (What does not kill me makes me stronger). This kind reaches out and into a person, that is, into the limits of a reader's imagination, by making a person aware of the limits not just of their own imagination but of the limits of the available thoughts by which she has to cognate what's been put forward. Put another way: these aphorisms are suggestive rather than prescriptive, though not less forceful. This structure of aphoristic writing *is itself* an argument against the kinds of writing for which there is only one kind of audience (that kind of writing might be analogous to the gaze singularly directed, implied, and so implicated by vanishing points, as Peggy Phelan described in *Unmarked: The Politics of Performance*), and for which there is only one kind of meaning-making.[1] Instead, it seeks to upend the reader from her position as a passive receiver, and so, upend the idea and the security of her oneness. We out here.

Seen this way, reading one kind of aphoristic expression means reading what the language points beyond, that is, a process of signification that is invested in pointing toward the limits of language and toward the space beyond what has been named. Its utterance, its performance, means to open rather than to close. In a way, the unrepresented field of potential meaning and action is constitutive of aphorism itself. This aphoristic, then, enacts the kind of intersubjectivity in its orientation toward the unfixity of the relation that a reader will bring to it. It is like the kind of seeing that takes the *unmarked* into account, that decenters the reading subject as a unitary, unified, reader-surveillant even as it asks us to be a part of its meaning-making, and makes us conscious of its invitation.

I waited outside the door to lay his clothes neatly on the bed until my grandmother told me he was in the shower and safely out of sight. It wasn't every morning. When he turned off the shower, she asked me to leave so I wouldn't see his stomach overpower his body onto the bed. The first thing that I learned about bodies was that they were not still.

Did that much body argue with itself, even while hugging some parts tightly and close like affection? And did some parts wrestle to be first, closest, farthest? How did skin, muscle, sinew, bone, and fat communicate? And who conceded first? Or could it be like art to decide who is on top, on the bottom, in the middle, like asking what the effect might be: just enough to be together, just enough to keep wondering. Did it matter who was looking? If there is an architect, what does it mean that there are no blueprints? Things like waves remind me of bodies, but I don't wince though (cruelty takes such small, practiced forms)—family is family (this one is a choice). His stomach grew over the bed when he lay down, and I liked how it kept changing shapes as he rolled over, sat up, stood. I see his stomach when I watch raw dough get folded into a cake pan—it piles up, then spreads out into cool, into calm, into flat.

On the bed, covered by a towel, he spread sideways, each part finding a place to rest and comfort itself. It escapes so much of the pageantry of depicted bodies, these tender edges laying supple against one another, being the same but amply so. The more delicate the skin, the more pale, until *pale* and *skin* seemed like the wrong words to use, the texture of the thinnest parts was so unlike the rest of him. Was it thin because it had to stretch? If he shrunk would it grow back thick and back like the other skin again? Is skin like rubber bands, pliable like imaginations?

Laying down, reaching his arms out, one breast falling neatly into the space where his armpit belonged but had been hidden over by how bodies can express time and old indulgences, and sometimes, the aftermath of bracing yourself from working at feverish paces for feverish years. His armpit was taken over by flesh that migrated from his chest and back and upper arm. In a middle school changing room before gym class was where I first encountered bowl-shaped armpits; it was like discovering alien bodies. Where did their arm go?

When he sat, even though it was harder to track under his clothes, his stomach found the side ways over his hips, reached down and out at the same time, growing into the seat next to him, forcing his arms wider. When he stood, his chest spanned sideways while it stretched down. The fabric of his shirt pinched and got hot. His arm must have felt irritated, where the fabric bit at loose skin with wrinkles and confusion. How could it not be impatient with fierce affection? He wrestled his arms over the top of his stomach when he crossed them, he grabbed for his elbows although he couldn't quite reach, even with his fingers extended and straining. Why try to keep any of it back or down? Something like this was not on James Baldwin's mind: "People are trapped in history and history is trapped in them."[2] It took me a long time to find the next question, because it can take a long time to hear all the ways a single thought can change how the world appears. Is it possible to mitigate harms while escaping and letting go? Are horizons—sometimes we clutch at them, sometimes they're in every scent—all that keep us alive in the meanwhile?

His pants also had to do work to keep him in, and to keep his upper and lower stomachs separate. All the while, the lower stomach might have begun to feel abandoned, and the upper stomach might have begun to think of the lower stomach as an imposter. There's a moment in the mornings when he pushed the lower stomach into place to zip up. I grew up to have a lower stomach and coaxed it into clothing, some days like dancing. There were times I had two different places where my back started and stopped, but it only mattered when I was sitting, and, even then, I didn't always notice. It is one way to understand how *plentitude* can masquerade as something else.

By accident, on those mornings, I saw that men have nipples, that they can have bigger nipples than women, that they can expand, that nipples can be different colors, that the same nipples can change colors. I liked that his were light brown when they were stretched out, and relaxed, seeming dark only by comparison with the rest of his chest's pale un-sun-kissed skin. ¡Mira éste, hasta se quema en la sombra! My mom badgered him for tanning so easily. For me, his pale skin promised the consistency of clouds, of blankets, of promises you know can't be kept but you believe them anyway and for as long as you can.[3] Then you find something else to believe and believe and believe and each time is a teacher of the need to become a part of *here*, and each break is a reminder you are not just *here*.

When he lifted any section of his stomach to scratch underneath, I could see the red, sore fold that marked a boundary, but I wasn't sure what it meant to have separate stomachs, unless my family was part cow, and Diaz wasn't kidding about curses that run through generations to mock maps and time and geography. There have been less likely things that have happened in human history, like Dippin' Dots, like Mickey Mouse, like Justin Bieber. I started to have red, sore folds to hide. I lost track of when they showed up from playing the game of trying to forget. Eventually, it was a forgetting game I called Hide and Keep that made it easier to believe with García Márquez in cyclical time, and made room for the magical thinking called empathy. But how to grow wider—making room for another—without becoming imperial? *I can be here with you* is half impossible, half untrue, and so often the only thing we need.

I liked looking at his hands pulling at the black curls on his head, the heavy joints and heavy fingers, heavy with gold rings and diamonds, heavy with heavy knuckles. That is what a capable hand looked like. I weighed the wide-link gold bracelet from his right wrist in my hands. It wrapped my whole palm in its circle. On the Ponte Vecchio in Florence, just outside compressed jewelry stores and their tiny gold treasures, my mother explained to my eleven years the wisdom: When the gold is heavy, that means it's a better quality.

After she ironed his pants—fresh each morning, of that much I'm sure—she brought them in, crisp, pleated, and warm. My dimpled hands smoothed over wool then khaki, as seasons changed. I decided I preferred wool but what I can't remember is how I knew to have a preference and stake a claim—it felt important to choose. In the comforting routine she taught me, pants became rectangles when I pinched from inside at the zipper just enough and again at the middle-back so that they became fit for pipes instead of legs, for people made of Legos instead of limbs. Like so much orderliness, this kind needed to forget whom the pants were for. I spread out his soft, white cotton under-shirt next to them.

Inspired by the idea of a system, I experimented with different ways of folding T-shirts. This was also a game to play. Down the middle, the long way first. Then, at the sleeves' seam. Then in half, with the sleeves neatly tucked away. I unfolded T-shirts that were folded incorrectly to make it right. I ar-ranged drawers by how long the sleeves were, and then arranged each pile ac-cording to the color wheel. Sometimes I started with white, sometimes with black, because not everything can be predetermined, except what comes af-ter a familiar first step. Wanting perfect creases stayed with me all the years I couldn't keep from packing up and moving on. Over time, I started to lose some of all the order I'd spent time inventing, and what's left is just how I fold T-shirts.

Laying across him watching television on the couch in the house where I lived until the summer I turned fourteen, where I prayed to the triangle of-fense, I reached for his mustache to push and pull and squeeze at the hair, coarse like a scrub brush, like it wouldn't move because it's been there forever or as long as my memory stretched, which was not the same thing but what does that matter when you are ten? I pulsed it between my first two fingers. The thickness surprised me, how bristles grouped together to be substan-tial and made mass. I didn't understand why hair has different textures, why softer hair doesn't grow on masculine faces. Or, why hair gets coarser with age and time, why I spent so much time thinking about my hair, smoothing it out of my face, orchestrating it into a pony tail, loosening it onto my shoul-ders, covering and uncovering my face, retreating, reappearing, debating its texture, how the gray hairs, when they began to sprout when I lived in Prince-ton for the part of graduate school that came before the second part of grad-uate school in California, why the gray hairs had unfamiliar kinks in them and why I wouldn't say, like he said about his own, that they are not silver, not gray, but platinum.

Often, he spent the night asleep on that couch, with the television flickering across his face, rumbling complaints into darkened air where I watched *Saved by the Bell*. The ritual of pinching then hiding pieces of hardened skin from

MAGICAL HABITS

my feet under the armrests left no account. Resentment, especially before I learned the word, could be a very quiet feeling, one I did not know I was having until it was something else, something creepier, a feeling passing by like a gentle ghost; I knew it had been there only when it vanished and I lived in its breeze.

When nighttime work had gone late and into morning, he didn't walk through the kitchen to the garage to go Downtown until the afternoon. Those days it smelled like his colognes and like Ultra SlimFast powder. There were years that they were all he drank. There were years of pretending food wasn't important. There were years that was more important than figuring out where the hunger came from. There were years of hidden appetites hiding. How to taste what's delicious and not need all of it at once.

I know what it sounds like when the blender devours ice, how quickly the ice gives in after its first, noisy fight. I hold the cover tight on top, how my grandma showed me. (I've started to dare the blender to erupt for no reason.) After all the ice was crushed and all the powder disappeared, it looked like a milkshake. I took a deep sip with a straw, and it was nothing like Eddy's milkshakes, the ones in tall, cold, steel containers like the spaceships in George Jetson's un-arrived future. I remember only two times I had milkshakes at Eddy's. The scoops of ice cream mixed with milk took as long as I took to drink them to melt. SlimFast was not thick and not creamy. In diet pill and exercise video infomercials I miss the lost years between before and after shots. "After" is an incomplete thought disguised as an end.

He didn't lie on the bed as long after a shower when he had a new shape, and he didn't stay as quiet. I kept his habit of lying on the bed in a towel to dry after a shower, as though weariness was testifying, and the question—because I was usually alone and so was he—was to whom.

An aphorism (a reason to keep writing them) can be a testimony from the future. A way to write as though we've already changed shapes. And the need to answer some questions has already vanished by being met. A body spreads into the bed to touch the sky.

AUGUST 2000 *Cambridge, Massachusett homelands*
REVISED FEBRUARY 2010 *Oakland, Ohlone homelands*
REVISED APRIL 2019 *Philadelphia, Lenni-Lenape homelands*

2002

"NO, NOT JUST the two of us, we're going to be ten for the brunch buffet—my daughter and her friends are on their way. Do you have a table closer to the food? Yeah, not that far in the back. Could we . . . what if we put those two tables in the middle together? Yeah, that's great, that's perfect, thank you so much. Thank you.

"¡Mi'ja! Hey, how are you? Hi, hey, nice meeting you. This is Prudenica, my wife. Hi. I'm Monica's dad. Hi, hello. Yeah, come sit down. I really enjoyed the concert last night. ¡Ja ja ja! Yes, I came to both. You saw me? Right, yeah I was in the front standing up. Oh yeah, it was great, Prudenica and I had a really good time. Real, real good time. And you just learned all that music this year? Did you all sing before?

"So it looks like they have a pretty good buffet. There's the lox platter; I know that's one of Monica's favorites. The salad station is over behind us. I had them sit us right by the dessert table, so make sure you save room. ¡Ja ja! What else did we see, Prudenica? We walked around a little bit, checking things out. There's an oyster bar—I don't know if you guys like oysters—and the jumbo shrimp actually look jumbo, which is nice. Sometimes, you know, they try to serve large shrimp and call them jumbo. They think we won't notice the difference. ¡Ja! It looks like they had a really nice roast beef they were slicing up, really juicy, not too much fat on it, and a roasted leg of lamb that looked juicy too. I might go have some of that, if Prudenica will let me. Eh, mi vida, what do you think? Are any of you guys vegetarians? There were some grilled vegetables and a vegetarian pasta I saw. If that's not enough, we can ask what else they have on the menu, just let me know. Are you sure that's enough? All right, you guys tell me; whatever you want, it's not a problem.

"And then, you know, they have all the other things you would expect at a brunch. What are you gonna get, mi'ja? I think I might go get myself a nice egg white omelet with spinach and onions from the omelet station. Maybe mushrooms. Oh, and they have waffles too. That I *know* Prudenica won't let me have, ¡Ja ja!

"White flour, and red meat mostly. Fried foods, oily foods. Not that much cheese, but once in a while. Not really pastas anymore. I know, when we were in Florence a few months ago it was really hard. But, it's okay. It's worth it. I was really bad. Remember?

"Do your friends know? How big I was? Aw, man! Yeah, that makes sense; I guess that doesn't come up. Prudenica saved me. She doesn't like to say that; she wants me to say that it was all me, that I'm the one who did it, that no one helped me. But that's how we met.

"Seriously! We met at the Pritikin Clinic. She was my personal trainer. ¡Ja ja ja! Yeah, we used to hang out on the treadmill. I would walk for like three hours a day. That's how I did it, all the weight, just by walking. Every day. And she would make me, even when I didn't want to. And there were lots of days I didn't want to. I was just real fucked up. She would hop on the treadmill next to me and walk with me. And we talked. That's all we did. We just talked the whole time while I was walking. She says she kept me talking so I could know if I was going too fast. ¡Ja! But yeah, I walked—we just walked.

"I don't know. Reina, what did we talk about?

"Months! A year, I think. It took me about a year and a half. One hundred and seventy-five pounds. I got down to one eighty-five. The doctor said that was too skinny, that it wasn't good for me. So now I'm about one ninety-five, one ninety-seven. Depending if I've been away from Prudenica or not. ¡Ja ja ja! She takes care of me. Prudenica takes care of me, right, Prudenica?

"Yeah, I know, just by walking. It's so simple! People get so concerned with what they should do and what they should and shouldn't eat. It's totally simple. Once I finally understood that, it was all possible. It's like a bank account. I need to take more calories out than I put in. That's it! All that other stuff, remember those SlimFast shakes I used to drink? All that stuff is bullshit. The reason that you lose weight when you're drinking those things isn't because you're drinking those things, it's because you aren't eating! I'm telling you, the amount of money I spent—even at the Pritikin Clinic. I only stayed there because I had no place to go, but then Prudenica let me come live with her.

Before we went to Groningen. How long, Prudenica? Like a year? Oh, about a year and a half we were over there. In her little apartment, ¡Ja ja ja!

"Like a bank account, that's right. So I just need to burn more calories than I take in. It's math. It's so simple. I eat fifteen hundred calories, burn more than that in a day, doing anything. And now they have so many gadgets and calorie counters, and things you can wear to count steps. It's so simple, I don't understand why more people don't just do it if they want to. Unless they don't want to, and I can understand that too. Well, there was a long time I just didn't give no fucking time to thinking about it. And I would get sick—I remember in San Diego, aw, man, I was in the emergency room, and I thought that was it. I thought that was really gonna be it. But I just didn't give a shit. I wanted what I wanted. But I didn't want this yet, ¡ja! Not yet. That took a long time, more wisdom. ¡Ja!

"We have this friend, she's a witch. She does readings of your energy. Have you ever had one? It's nuts; well, she's a little nuts. But she's real good people. Real, real good. I don't know what I think of reading people's energy; it's a little bit out there. But she brought her friend over; he's famous for being a visionary or something. I don't have no idea what she's talkin' about half the time, right, Prudenica? But he's famous for being able to see energy. So he saw my chakras (my chakras!) when we met him. That's what he called them: chakras. I have seven, and he said I had an extra one. I don't know, everyone has one on top of their head, but he said I had an extra one, and that the one on top of my head was really bright. It's supposed to be white, and he said mine was one of the biggest and brightest he'd seen. I don't have no idea! But that's what he said. That it was big, and bright, and bee-yoo-tee-ful! Right, Prudenica?"

5. heartbreak as praxis

En el Valle de México el hombre se siente suspendido entre el cielo y la tierra y oscila entre poderes y fuerzas contrarias, ojos petrifica-dos, bocas que devoran. La realidad, esto es, el mundo que nos ro-dea, existe por sí misma, tiene vida propia y no ha sido inventada, como en los Estados Unidos, por el hombre. El mexicano se siente arrancado del seno de esa realidad, a un tiempo creadora y de-structora, Madre y Tumba. Ha olvidado el nombre, la palabra que lo liga a todas esas fuerzas en que se manifesta la vida. Por eso grita o calla, apuñalea o reza, se echa a dormir cien años.—OCTAVIO PAZ, *El laberinto de la soledad*

I KEEP AN eight-by-ten of four-year-old me in my study, from when I was so chatty that my great aunt Teresa called me Periquita. A portrait of a little para-keet. I'm in pigtails, high on both sides, the middle part struggling with the cowlicks along my hairline. A too-precious pink rose with light green leaves perches near a corner of the bigger-than-my-head white triangle collar, lined with scalloped lace. The dress is navy blue with white polka dots and puff sleeves to the elbow; half-chubbed arms (little round hand over round little hand) rest carefully on my lap—but my lap didn't make it into the shot. Just as I do now, I lower my chin to look up at the lens, as though I've just come out from under a secret. But I might not tell you what it is.

There are nights and nights she's watching me, and I am watching a com-puter screen, listening to its tight breath.[1] My generation started listening like breathing to computers in high school, and it's been at least since Nietz-

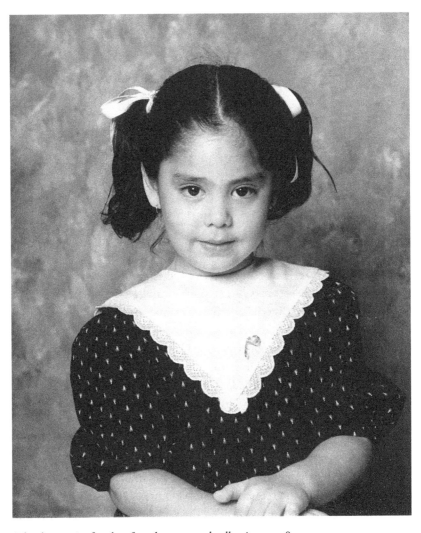

School portrait of author from her personal collection, c. 1985.

sche noticed the modern tendency to be wrapped in a quickening world that we've wondered whether we'd be able to digest at a speed that matched our machines.[2] Where would there be to be quiet anymore? Or did we never really need silence the way we need water, to survive? Or, in a world of noise, was there something else quiet could be for? After all, so many secrets (hidden under, inside, beside silences) were an excuse for someone to tell us who we were and what or whom to adore. Does freedom look exactly like all of us, after all? And like noise instead?

MAGICAL HABITS

Instead of whatever else I might be doing, I might be falling in love, sometimes while the guitarrón and Vicente Fernández insist they know how to lose and would die if I'd only let them return. That song could be someone else's craving. I have no way of tracing it—unless I count the times I recoiled at it while eating gorditas en la veintiséis, or waiting for my mom to finish the bookkeeping, or huddled in the corner of an equipal in Cancún. No matter. When he or Ana Gabriel or Lola Beltrán or Juan Gabriel sing "Volver" it sounds like what I've been waiting for, like it could explain something. It's the last thing I would have ever guessed at fourteen: that I return to this song on purpose. Return to the song that insists on return to return to where I've never and ever been, as though I'm its vanishing point.

It is how mariachi songs tend to begin and where they, in turn, return at the very beginning: a grito with no story yet attached (and so every story is attached and can attach). Octavio Paz called it the most Mexican sound. And with all due respect, I have several cousins who would disagree. What's a Mexican sound?, they would say, What makes it Mexican? Is crying and lament really a Mexican thing? Or they would play me music I don't listen to because the loves I return to are Sam Cooke, D'Angelo, and Prince. After all, the reason I read Paz in college in the first place was to find words and ideas like el grito, since I didn't know if I could ever convincingly make the sound. It turns out I can. But I wouldn't bet that that's about my ancestral spirit or blood.

An ethnomusicologist might write: A grito is pitched high, and pushed out powerfully, diaphragmatically against the air. The first sound might begin by catching the back of the throat, as the tongue glides away from teeth, pulling the lips almost into a smile. The pitch reaches beyond and over the trumpets, and the throat closes over the sound sharply only to open, to close, to open, the clipped effect as though between exhilaration and pain. It makes a body masculine enough to hold despair and torment until both are beautiful again. And it makes masculinity capacious enough to lay claim to visceral, soul-rending agony, only in order to pretend to enjoy controlling it. The rapture of being caught up by the surrender you choose.

The sound, when you make it, means like aching but feels really, really good. Plainly put, it's an erotic eruption. In an outside/inside Mexican Catholicism there are other points of arrival than the ones where you hurt because you deserve it, pledging allegiance to suffering (mine or yours) as if it earns worth, and where if you hurt there's only mourning. Here's the assurance, which is also a wager: emotional worlds are not lived out as taxonomy, one at a time.

-- ➡

In 1962, a friend offered Emeterio Gutiérrez an unbeatable deal: the Nuevo León restaurant for the price of the kitchen equipment. Only five thousand dollars. Fifty-some years later, Emeterio's son, Daniel, and his son, Daniel Jr., still operate the restaurant. For Daniel Gutiérrez Sr., what kept Nuevo León restaurant Mexican is that its menu remains the same as it was in 1962. He explains, "There's a way to cook. . . . I try to put that flavor all the time. . . . I have to be steady with employees. . . . It's like a friend of mine who owns a restaurant and he says, 'Danny, let's not make things bigger, let's make things better.' We're considered, our restaurant here for forty years, we're considered one of the most consistent restaurants in the city, probably in the United States."[3]

For Gutiérrez, Nuevo León's success is about its consistency. In the 1990s, after almost thirty years of consistency, Nuevo León began to receive local and national awards for its food. But Gutiérrez could also think of his food as getting "better" at the same time that it remained consistent—in a sense, in opposition to the "make it bigger" American credo. While Nuevo León's food aspired to consistency, Gutiérrez's personal story displays much more dynamism.

When asked about his life, Gutiérrez shifts between seeing himself as foreign and clearly belonging in and to Chicago. But he doesn't worry about any tensions or contradictions.[4] Gutiérrez envisions himself as existing physically within but psychologically outside the United States: "I know we're in a country that doesn't belong to us. We're from Mexico."[5] Here, he defines his identity in terms of national origin, simplifying and "forgetting" the realities of migration that he himself lived through. For Gutiérrez, this "forgetting" contextualizes the difficulties of migrating to the United States in particular, where he endured being called an "enchilada kid."[6] Gutiérrez's narration of himself in an ongoing relation with Mexico also became a way to imagine himself as unequivocally belonging somewhere, even if it wasn't the place he lived. During our conversation, he ultimately dismissed his childhood memories as unimportant and simply a "part of life." But through that same childhood, through his marriage and family, and through his service in the army, later in the conversation, he claimed to be "a part of this country."[7]

Yes, I am a part of this country, because I was raised here, I could probably say that I was raised here. . . . They ask me where you are from, I'm from Chicago, I don't say I'm from Mexico no more, I've been here forty-five years. I was raised here, I got married here, I had four . . . three daughters and a son, I got eight grandkids, where are you from, I say here. . . . I know that I am not originally from here, but I am from Mexico; but, hey, I went to school here, I went to the army here, I raised my kids here, I got married here.[8]

What else would "here" need in order to be from it? The contradiction between being "from Mexico" and being "a part of this country," the insistent "here" in his story, crystallizes the choice Gutiérrez makes between different stories he could tell. From how he chooses to tell his personal history, it's difficult to reconstruct place as a kind of stability.

The overlapping declarations—at times rejecting and at other times claiming Mexico—are not evidence of nostalgia. Because Gutiérrez believes both these narratives to be true, remaking the past in the present through available grammar is about a perceived or felt emotional need to connect to a national geography. Yet those needs supersede the idea of national geographies and the bureaucracies and armies that enforce maps and passports. The idea of Mexico gives him what the idea and experience of the United States cannot and vice versa. His is some other map.

The glossy cover of Nuevo León's menu reproduces exactly this logic: a yellow structure snuggles in front of the looming John Hancock Building and Sears Tower. A sign reads *Nuevo León* in purple script over the brown door of the bright building. While Nuevo León is clearly placed in Chicago through two of its most notable architectural landmarks, large cacti frame the restaurant and disrupt the iconic skyline. Fluorescent pink and yellow, Nuevo León's building contrasts against the skyscrapers' more muted shades. Behind the restaurant, a brown wooden fence and a row of little houses set a boundary between the city and the restaurant. Nuevo León remakes the metropolis through bringing symbols like the cacti meant to evoke a sense of "Mexico" to the city. The glowing colors and cacti curiously tower over the restaurant and seem to pronounce Mexicanness almost in and as excess. So that while the menu claims Chicago as the setting for the restaurant, it attempts to fix and even overdo Mexicanness with fiesta colors and desert symbols.

Inside the menu, a Gutiérrez family portrait does work similar to yet distinct from the cacti in guaranteeing the Mexicanness of the food. A prominent portrait of María Gutiérrez, Emeterio's wife, and her sons, Antonio, Emeterio Jr., Daniel, and Raul, displays the family to represent an unchanging and singular sense of Mexicanness. The domestic sphere often symbolizes the stability of tradition; this family picture in the menu likewise creates an image of unchanging Mexicanness. Yet, there are no obvious ethnic markers in the portrait: all four children have their dark hair cut similarly short; they each wear a button-down shirt with a collar. María Gutiérrez, with three children standing in front of her and the eldest standing behind her, wears a dark dress with small white polka dots. The image was originally a black-and-white photo. It is the caption, "Familia Gutiérrez," that marks the ethnicity of the family.[9] This Mexicanness authenticates the food, supporting the message that it comes from a family of "real Mexicans." Additionally, the background color of the portrait has been changed to match the burgundy of the menu's border. This alteration of the original image helps integrate it with the menu so that, together, words and images produce a single, coherent account. It is an effort to create the Mexicanness of the menu as consistent with the Mexicanness asserted by the family portrait. But what the image strains to claim and verify arises not only from the caption and graphic design but from the narratives of family origin that follow the portrait, one in Spanish and one in English.

Captioned "Un Poquito de Historia" and "A Bit of History," the two stories recount the family's migration to Chicago in the 1950s: María and Emeterio Gutiérrez "migrated to Chicago, in search of a better life for themselves and their growing family. . . . They both struggled and worked hard to maintain their family."[10] The story is familiar: one about becoming successful through hard work, about how America is a uniquely open society in which a family might do that. The idea of a "better life" is measured in strictly and strenuously economic terms: hard work and its storied rewards. Similarly, the short story about the Gutiérrez family emphasizes the struggle that has to come before life could be better. Life, one gets the sense, would never count as better without the struggle.

At the same time, Nuevo León is referred to as their "native land." But the adjective doesn't quite work. Nuevo León as the "native" land would make Chicago foreign territory.[11] But the story asks us to believe that Chicago is also a place the family belongs by way of the restaurant's history. Chicago—or, at least, aiming for a home and better life in Chicago—is the beginning of the story, even as it is still a destination. Mexico is already a memory here, even though the titles "Un Poquito de Historia" and "A Bit of History" bring Mexico along in a way that is important for making the food Mexican in Chicago. Still, this claim to history is in some ways a very twentieth- and twenty-first-century way of belonging to a nation expressed through settler national sovereignty. Declaring a "native" land other than Chicago after forty years of living in Chicago, while at the same time believing that new homes can be made and earned in Chicago, for one thing disrupts any easy notion of belonging, where all one's feelings need to make a kind of "sense" according to settler colonial geography.

⸻

But if there *is* something to listen for that I can call mine, how is anyone supposed to move if every beginning aches? Might I always be out of joint with time?—the way the guitarrón pulls back even on "El Polvorete," a song that insists on a fairy tale: that no hawk will ever catch up to eat the dove. Songs like these are the only training I can think of that prepared me for living in America and not because I've ever lived anywhere else. We all need primers and guidebooks on how to live in (spite of) America, a living that—if it's going to be honest—has to begin if it's going to begin with heartbreak. Any other beginning is a romance. Not so far from Mexico, after all.

One problem is that we haven't figured out how to talk about Google Chat conversations and text messages, as though we didn't fall in love that way too, with dots that turn green only (how to help thinking?) for me—when maybe it was their pet skimming past the keyboard looking for affection—and with three-dotted bubbles that turn bright and blue, like they turn the whole world on. It's tender to admit.

We think up the sound of voices and store and then replay them, hold and retell them, even though we saw them only that one time. Instead of transporting us to some spiritless place we've never been, our beloved technologies keep bringing us back to conjuring ghosts from thin air and tight breaths that might as well be the wind, not because they are empty but because they are always here.

But it's not the 1990s anymore, and we've found our way to the other end of a rabbit hole. First, Tom Hanks and Meg Ryan made it okay for everyone to date online. Then, Facebook and Google gentrified the internets together, in a world where what's normalized as safe and sensible is what makes the fewest people the most profit. But if we're banking on romance happening there, too, to imagine we can escape our bodies and come back to them, it's worth noting it's the same impulse as when Oliver Wendell Holmes Sr. imagined his spirit took a little trip to a place he'd never been when he looked at a stereograph.[12] Really nothing makes us believers in magic quicker than our own machines.

Often, through no one's fault exactly, the connection cuts off. That muffled, tortured dial-up connection song warned us there were cracks, instabilities, confusions ahead. But then again, maybe it's this simple: it is genuinely hard to feel responsible to an idea, a hint, a good feeling I felt in a room of my own at three in the morning, while the weather changed outside. That's how I understand it when the story of falling in love with flashing dots, bubbles, and opaque windows ends in the normal way, with a disappearance or a faint-hearted send-off. What I really wish is that my rituals of leaving would have generated by now some form of inoculation—and yet, and yet. The songs begin with un grito.

I've taken stock of the endings, the endings that often began when I moved somewhere else, subject to a restlessness that's just as much structural as intellectual as emotional as visceral as ancestral as physiological. A cumulative review. And usually just in time for spring, just as I've been used to packing up for somewhere new, I succumb to the old habit, the one that works between prayer and exorcism, a series of incantations seeking out the promise of catharsis: to empty out. But without Aristotle's need for fear or pity, without the need to become either pure or Athenian (not, of course, that he or any Greek citizen would have invited me to the theater). Only honest. What's the right aphorism for how heart-wrenching it can be to keep being honest, alongside the way your terms for understanding the world, people, history, chance morph? We out here.

I fell in love once with someone who was in love with biology. He believed its promises of a solution just beyond the next set of variables the way I put stock in the persistence of mysteries even when the stories add up. Not even because I am drawn toward mysticism. But because the most material accounting of our stories—and there's no knowledge that isn't bound up with stories—promises that, eventually, they all show their edges. A sliver of a slip peeking out from a skirt that grows too short over time, that shrunk in the dryer, or that frayed with use.

But that's not what he thought. He nurtured the idea of systems that balance like Jenga on principles so simple he could list them. Perhaps this is the first masculine yearning, the first principle of masculinity, that principles can somehow solve and resolve the entire world. It was in organic chemistry in college when I started thinking it was beautiful, he said.

That summer he was about to finish medical school. I bought Crayolas and coloring books and spent days staying in the lines, adding Laser Yellow suns and blades of grass with Magic Mint highlights in the blank spaces, lounging together in Sheep's Meadow. He took off his shoes, walked alone to the center of the green; he said something about, The grass between my toes makes me feel peaceful. We played word games between kissing: First one who couldn't think of another animal's name that started with the letter D lost. I won with

MAGICAL HABITS

dragon but had to fight for it. He didn't think to say *dinosaur*. Another day, I left his apartment abruptly, late for dinner, the way dinners in New York might as well be scheduled meetings, still flushed and buttoning, smoothing my hair up while I waited for the elevator and to catch my breath. A part of me stayed in the park, and another inside against the wall, both times asking whether he could play again the next day.

When the lunar nodes of two people in a relationship line up, my astrologer told me, it can feel like you've always known each other and like you suddenly found someone else who speaks your secret language.

We found each other the next year on one of Berkeley's perfect hills overlooking the Bay Bridge and watched the sky behind it turn Carnation Pink. He said, It's like this: when we're talking, it's like we're alone together in a room with no windows. He was trying to solve why he'd decided to be with someone that wasn't me, and I was equally committed to the mystery. Wait, I wanted to know, Why can't there be a window? What if I get claustrophobic? He laughed, Okay, there can be a window, but it's in the corner. The point is no one can see us and we can't see them. It's just us and we're in there, and there's a game only we know, and we play it. It's great. I love it. And when we finish we stand up and go back home. He was trying to make it simple but I was pretty sure the last thing I needed was a metaphor. It was the season he was figuring out where and what he wanted home to be, the way twenty-nine-year-olds do, and I'd already made up my mind. Then you left to California, he said, with a hint of accusation. Right, I answered, you were moving here a month later.

I wished him a happy birthday with an extended meditation on the number twenty-nine, and the next summer, and again with every move, the crayons pop up to remind me of the ones who mistake their metaphors and mind puzzles for generosity.

Some other times it was someone who thought what the "republic of the spirit" needed was a king—one like Jesus, one of music, one of pictures, one of freedom.

Like many privileged, nerdy people, college for me was about conversations that pushed at the other person's seams until dawn, and I wanted to fight all the fights at once because they were all winnable. His Jesus (a different one from my inside/outside Catholic one) was a good adversary for me, and he was training to be a lawyer, so he needed practice. We both graduated from Harvard with a five-year plan, and the last time we walked together out of the Yard, it was beside all the other confident five- and ten-year plans.

I left to spend the summer in Costa Rica with a friend who wanted to learn to surf. I wanted to learn how to flirt with a boogie boarder. When you left to Costa Rica, Jesus spoke to me. There's an important verse for us that says we should not be unequally yoked. What? But I've been going to church with you. I prayed about it with my prayer group, and you aren't baptized. There are facts not worth fighting over or contextualizing or finessing even if it's unavoidable how they are attached to stories and vantage. Before I deleted my account, we wrote "Happy Birthday!" to each other on Facebook, three days apart. As luck would have it, we really mean it.

Some theories lock away what they'd rather not wrestle with or be unsettled by. Another way of reading them is to ask what their elegant architectures have to pause to keep them upright: sometimes it's entire peoples, sometimes it's history, sometimes it's the force of uncertainty, sometimes it's the distances and dimensions between you and me.

When I was twenty-five, I trusted the fact that he could hear all the space hidden inside quiet and make it dance with a drum set. Really, my unoriginal devotion to talent is just the shape my narcissism takes, but I used to think it was a great virtue. In the evening, before playing jazz downtown all night and until dawn, he rubbed my feet and stretched out my hamstrings. He was the first to notice my IT bands were unusually tight, and that it had to do with how my hips are set unevenly in their joints. He ran track in high school in Houston and could tell my legs were different lengths while he stretched them out. He made the best fried chicken and potato salad I've ever had, and we talked, sincerely, about raising our children in Brooklyn. I moved to California, and there was no way either then or now to be sure, even by asking, but I think he held it against me. We never wished each other happy birthday.

Another one felt like looking into a kaleidoscope: the spiky patterns morphing into other spiky patterns making me dizzy when I turned it. Older Black women love me—I just know how to make them happy, he said. What does that even mean? I know how to make them like me. Isn't that a version of being manipulative? No. Why wouldn't I make someone happy if I knew how to do it? Yeah, that *sounds* reasonable, but it matters that you're making them happy according to some formula, *so that* they'll like you. Doesn't everyone do that? Don't you do things because you know they will make your friends happy? Sure, but that's not the basis of our entire relationship, it's part of it. Right, well it's part of it for me too, but a bigger part. You're a ridiculous person who is good at sounding like a reasonable person.

He said I asked too many questions, and there wasn't much to say after that because I do, and then so what?

I asked, How can I know what you're feeling if I don't ask questions? I don't have feelings. Well, I have one. Intercourse. But that's basically a bunch of little high fives with your genitals.

We were driving back to New York weeks later, he said, I was telling you about how aware I am in every situation of being Black and how I can't help thinking about people's perceptions of me because of that. You kept asking questions, wanting to go deeper, when I didn't think there was anything else to think about. But I wasn't asking questions about being Black or being conscious of other people's perceptions of that. I mean, I was at first, but then I was asking whether you could imagine the possibility that *for someone else* how he or she was perceived could not matter in a moment, like even if they knew it was going on and inevitable. I totally understood what you were saying, you know I've thought about exactly that my entire life, but I was asking whether in your imagination there was any space at all for something else, even only in the hypothetical—like, could someone else choose to *not* keep wondering, even if they knew it would always, always happen? And *then*, after that, I was curious about what thoughts in general felt like to you, like whether there are ever sensations attached to them for you; I was going to tell you that there are for me, but that's when you stopped listening because you wanted me to stop talking. *But*, to be extra clear, those last ones weren't about anyone being Black, they were about what's intimate about thinking and the fact that thinking can be part feelings, part sensations, part memory, part openness, part who knows, part like listening—that thinking is an experience too. Or you could have told me that being Black was part of how you feel that stuff too. There's no winning with you. Then why are you fighting me? I missed his last birthday and texted a belated cake emoji. He said it tasted just like regular cake emoji.

I also tried out being in love with a white man. He called himself a Communist. His Catholic, military family had landed in the Carolinas after a series of nearly annual moves that no one chose. They recited them to one another—like a litany—as often as I was around, placing each memory in the sequence, over and again. Before New Bern, before O'Fallon, after Fresno, before Yuma. Cumulative review.

He also thought I asked too many questions, like about the tiny statue of Mao on his bookshelf, there with pictures of Frederick Douglass, Nina Simone, and a votive candle emblazoned with Prince Rogers Nelson's image that I bought him for Christmas. Portraits of the Communist fathers were likewise arranged around his house like a baseball card collection on display. Another kind of litany.

He liked to say things. He liked to say he'd learned from the Black feminists he'd read in college that love was a verb.[13] Love is a verb, turned into a slogan, the way you might attach to a good idea, decide it's decided and obvious what it means, and never let go. He liked to say his favorite words: *strategy, provocative, sophisticated, efficient, effective,* and *the dils.* He liked to say his organizing work had a theory of change. He explained the "mass line" to me fifty times, as though it were scripture and handed me Mao's "Combat Liberalism."

We meet the question every generation: Is there another way to insist on otherwise possibilities than through claiming that change begins with any kind of certainty? Isn't there a tender allegiance among a theory, a hope, questions, works of imagination, and speculation—and a deep-sea distance between a theory and control, between a theory and a fetish, when the fetish feels good to say? (Provocative.) Isn't the clearest horizon to give back all this land and ordain reparations, and to concede that neither you nor I should make any clean decisions about how that should go? Aren't there freer worlds, not just freer than this one, freer than any father could imagine? Marx, after all, could not quite get a handle on desire's dark and light work in the world, so distinct from bare necessities, and never far from either motivation or joy. Isn't a huge portion of some other world the moment when the loudest ones—the ones who like to say things—become quiet and listen? Do people only fight for their lives if they have a script to slice up the world? Is that the source of our highest courage? Or is it the capacity to turn history inside/outside and insist there is space yet?

He liked to say some tantrums as declarations: People tell me I am the best listener they've ever met. When I need to talk, for as long as I need to say things, you have to listen and you and your face have to stay quiet; when I'm done, the one thing you can say is you can say you believe me. I get a lot of positive affirmation about the person I am in the world. You know you have to kiss me when I want to kiss you, or I will be upset. Everyone tells me how great I am at relationships. I don't want to be with someone who thinks they know me better than I know myself. I am really great at relationships. When you ask questions you're questioning my character.

He liked to say his prayer: as long as I know what the boundaries are, then I can feel free inside them.

Stories—even calcified ones—ask questions by asking that questions be asked: How did you get here? And how did I get there? What were the contingencies, one by one, and what are the instincts by name and affection? What did you come by honestly, and dishonestly, and through manipulation, and due to overexposure or underexposure or simple—though not innocent— exposure? How can you tell the difference between choice and unchoice, when only some parts can be options? Is that masochism, martyrdom, liberation? Will you recognize yourself if you grow beyond the boundaries you can name, the allegiances you made when you were twenty? Should you grow anyway? Can you let go of the stories, even the ones that brought you here and kept you safe? What is beyond safe safety? When is the precise moment a story can become a myth, a straightjacket, sickness, an echo anticipating falling apart before it happens, because you've metabolized the rhythm of falling apart—city by city—as though it's steadiness? What is obedience, what is reverence, what is addiction? What is it called when you shred something holy you love (shredding, after all, is a verb too), and can we agree this is not freedom? Can you feel and see it, all of this, can it all be withstood? Can you fit it all where it needs to go when it needs to go? Do you have a name for it before you go, do you just go? What is and how to balance doing always doing ever doing trying to do trying to perform to repeat a script of love for freedom, these precise, exact steps, written on butcher paper with a Sharpie in the kitchen, every kitchen someone invites you to, the same steps, one, two, three, small groups, four, five, six, circle up, positive affirmation—how to balance it with being, just being, the simple, solemn, quiet being of *free* if you can taste it, if you can touch it, in a moment, a sip of lemonade, the crackle of a fire burning down the last jail, moments you don't know will happen even when you dream them, that can only happen in their way if you don't try to control every certain detail of how they might and yet insist with everything beyond certainty (almost everything), because nothing is new under the sun and nothing ever quite repeats? Is there space for the world to come and meet you even on the best of days to surprise you if you listen to ten albums on repeat on repeat to talk about ten movies on repeat on repeat to make everyone you know talk about the four things you love through memorizing them? Isn't that, after all, what you're really looking for: some world you don't already know?

For historian Carolyn Steedman, one of Freud's clearest representations of the death drive comes in "Beyond the Pleasure Principle," as the compulsion to repeat.[14] Cordoning off otherwise possibilities through repetition—thereby extinguishing even the idea of possibility—does not, itself, end life. Instead, repetition is a self-enforced limit on life and liveliness. Even a genre is most "alive" when its conventions slant. Some habits—repetition—save you in a moment by helping you make sense of a moment, get through the parts of a moment that outlast a moment. They lend the comfort of security and control's warmest fictions: that control is real outside the violence of enforcement. So then here is another horizon: the same habits that in a moment saved you can become—in another moment, if you repeat them often enough, if you repeat them to make sure the world can't grow or change your understanding of them, or you, and why you need them and love them and keep them even a little too long—a trap.

❧

Each time it happens in that ordinary way. How helpful would it be if we'd decided heartbreak rhymed with the way the breeze catches or doesn't catch a sail on a tilted and spinning earth, instead of with tragedy, especially when the heart beats feminine? Love stories should adapt, the way beast fables became children's stories when the king needed a way to order a confusion of dimension, distance, and demography according to the Number One, the way everyday gods and stones became Religion.[15] Each time, you glimpse the philosophers' dilemma of building the whole world from braiding thoughts together and dedicating lifetimes to proving that only those careful strands exist—leaving small, hidden alcoves for accidents and earthquakes, confused by which part you made up, who made you do it, or did you choose to. This is the marriage between philosophy and masculinity; in any body you're in, you can take it on or leave it. To mourn the falling leaves or leave their memories where they fall.

Along with everything else there might be, there's rest (a quiet form of freedom) in the idea that some words will never settle down to be singular—*choice*, *mine*, *knowing*—no matter how much time passes or doesn't pass, no matter how many cities I can list that I've lived in, or people I decide to love. If a horizon is a risk, it's also a promise, and I need both to breathe. Not to own or control anything. It's not dogma. Enmeshed in the workings of horror, murder, and inequity, breathing is a verb, which continues as choice and not choice too.[16] At least so long as we have the sky.

❧

I care, so I'm shy to admit I've thought about it for a long time. These are still machines, even if they are slicker, even if they seem to obey our subtle touch, our careful pinch, like a lover.[17] Even when they—lovers and machines—take much more from us than touch. How long we are at the screen, how our fingers glaze over the absent keyboard, the words we tend to use, how many steps in a day, our mood, our sleep, our schedule, caloric intake, travel plans. Somehow (it's the hope) we'll digest it all—or else get eaten up (it's the ghost story).

Lovers and cannibals and technologies share more than a few strands of DNA. I've needed the myths they proffered like a training montage in a sports movie, to practice knowing their differences and meeting grounds. A practice in turning history inside/outside. But stomachs don't need anything like old words or new stories, just a way of breathing into them.

AUGUST 2003 *Cambridge, Massachusett homelands*
REVISED MAY 2020 *Philadelphia, Lenni-Lenape homelands*

monica huerta
TUE, MAY 10, 2011, 1:05PM
TO: *****@gmail.com

it's actually this really unbalanced number, and threes and nines are even my favorite. 19 makes more sense, and so does 39 (odd number with odd number, keeping each other company). but the perfect symmetry of the 2, next to the 9, which if you try to make symmetry out of will always leave you either with extra or with halves. like the number knows it's the moment before something that can't be anticipated, how we know change is happening exactly when we lose a bit of balance.

it (29) has felt, most days, like standing on the edge of a cliff, in the best sense, or, a few nights ago in a dream, i was at the helm (it's unclear why i know the word "helm" or that its appropriate to use here; a few weeks ago at trivia i inexplicably knew the names of a bunch of breeds of dogs; cellular memory, yo. it's real.)--but anyway, i was at the helm of a ship in the dream--the duck boat taxi had transformed into an 18th century schooner, no one knows why--and it was crashing almost straight down into the ocean, my body parallel to the waves. and it was my choice to either be mesmerized or terrified, to keep my eyes open and accepting, or closed, resisting.

it's really a choice we're always making--do we let life in or shut it out? and which parts?--but at 29, the consequences of choosing the latter (shutting out), for me, have felt most explicit. one of my favorite lines from a movie, "que dejamos atras cuando cruzamos fronteras?" [what do we leave behind when we cross borders?] is the choice put in motion. i love the shuffle of it, and it makes me nervous. my deeper self wishes for safety, my growing self knows to reach out for more than that, that there can be more risk, sometimes, in staying perfectly still: what to keep, what to leave behind, what to keep, what to leave behind. what's mine, what's inheritance, what's ancient, what's mine, what's family, what's blood, what's duty, what's mine. And--the best i've got--is that growing up and older doesn't mean more answers, just more peace with questions. or at least, that's the goal i aim for :)

for your birthday--happy birthdaaaaaaaaaaaaaaaaayyyyyyyyyyyyyyyyy!!!!!!!!--a thought: maybe in the corner of the room you're flying in, you're not trying to get at some errant dust (could you tell from my face this wasn't super convincing for me? my face is a terrible liar). maybe, just maybe, in the corner, you are looking for a window. (no judgment on the fact that you don't understand that, structurally, it probably wouldn't make sense to put a window in the corner.)

wishing you the happiest of birthdays, the sunniest of days, and lots of that kind of shade to lie under that palm trees give when the breeze is just right and the sun flickers, in patterns, past the leaves.

always good things and pie.m

ps: after i saw you last, as if the universe heard my/our yearning, i was greeted at the birthday bbq with the *most* delicious, the *most* moistestestest chocolate cake--with strawberries on top and inCREDIble chocolate icing. it was proof of something, i just know it. i don't know of what, but PROOF. proof, i tell you. that the world listens attentively when you say with your whole self, "moist cake. nothing in the whole wide world like moist, chocolately heaven cake." so i also wish you cake.

6. whether wisdom

The aesthetic turn here is not, however, a mere empty formalism;
it is, rather, an affective reworking, an immanence, transforming reading into an ascetic practice of self-emptying.
—STEPHEN BEST, *None Like Us: Blackness, Belonging, Aesthetic Life*

THERE WAS AN ALCOVE in their bedroom—in the house where I learned
to play the flute, then stopped. It was in their bedroom, but habit made the
alcove mine. Rarely did I stay for long, but two pieces of furniture kept me
company: a coffee table, always too far from me, its legs slouching under
the weight of mine, my calves sticking to it, the backs of my knees straining
from the distance. The creamy leather, on what I learned much later to call
a chaise, stretched past the point of comfort. But when I sat there, however
uncomfortably, the whole world went quiet and still.

I boasted to friends who asked if the wood of the tall, dark headboard in
the room was painted that the wood is *inlaid* and from Sorrento, Italy, on the
Amalfi Coast. There are phrases children learn to say, not just the words but
the tone, to take on an entire mood they might not yet be able to claim but
rather into which they grow. I felt like an expert, and worldly, like it was real
that I'd seen glass blown by hand in Venice, and heard Hungarians ooh! and
aah! at fireworks on New Year's Eve, had apple tea in Istanbul, spent my thir-
teenth birthday in Haifa, Israel, and compared the blue of the Mediterranean
to the blue of the domes dotting the Greek island of Mykonos. I snuck all
those trips into that one word, *inlaid*, and hoped I also conveyed that time the
violins played for my birthday dinner in Rome. I had a sense that not every
eleven-year-old goes on vacation to Indonesia and Morocco. In another way,

it made me upset that we never visited the Grand Canyon, or learned how to ski, and could not find Lake Tahoe. I thought it could have made me calmer, or happier, or fitter; it was Colorado and Myrtle Beach that were exotic.

This is the house where three bay windows looked out onto the backyard, the pool, and an empty plot of land (which was rare in that part of the cul-de-sac suburbs of Chicago), just in front of what I called a forest. I imagined the isthmus cradled all the sorcery in the world, and I wanted very badly to believe that, had I been able to stand the fear, I could have figured out that at the other end of the lake, beyond a thicket of pine trees, was another two-story house, with a bean-shaped pool, just like ours. When I check Google Maps now, the empty plot and forest are gone, and I even discovered later on that the forest was a planted plot of trees, not a hundred yards deep, not then ten years old, and what I had called a lake was just the imprint of some particularly soggy Aprils. But some childhood visions and decisions are too thick to see through, so I still see a forest and the empty plot, magically out of place and meant specifically for me to run my imagination over. As far as I'm concerned, the forest stays a forest, sorcery keeps its home, and there are worse things than being that stubborn, if I can remember it's my stubbornness that keeps them in place.

This is the house where I listened to all the early 1990s music I perform with everyone who's inclined at karaoke. The house with the leather sectional full of bits of resentment, the high ceilings that made me want to be an opera singer so I could fill them up, before I knew *Phantom of the Opera* was not an opera, or that the difference matters to anyone, or that it would start to matter a little (but only a very little and up to a point and in some contexts and not others) to me. I think it is the saddest story and still cry when I hear "The Music of the Night" because I know how it ends, and I know that it will, and I would like very much to stop it and give the Phantom some time to change his mind.

This is also the house where I started loving villains and learned to play the flute in the room across the blue-tiled Jack and Jill bathroom from my sister's room. I took it when she left for college—before she left college before "finishing"—and then regretted it because, unlike my old room, its morning sunlight was cutting and bright. When I lived in the darker room, with the burnt orange and deep green leaf-patterned quilt I grudgingly endured, I sat on one of the beds, the one that wasn't where my grandmother prayed the rosary over me every night. She prayed while sitting on my feet the way I asked her to, the way that becomes the reason I want heavy blankets to cover me, even in Brooklyn's and Jersey's mid-August heat. Eventually, I buy a weighted blanket.

In that darker, leaf-patterned room, this is how I practice the flute in the house that is the house of all the childhoods I can remember, the one I left as I was turning fourteen: I close both doors—the one to the bathroom, the one to the hallway—and sit on the leaf pattern, lay the music in front of my crossed legs. Fingering. Scales. Scales with my eyes closed. Scales backward. Whole note scales. Quarter note scales. Half note scales. Dotted half note scales. Scales in 4/4 time, in 3/4 time, in 6/8. I learn the trick is hearing counting when it's quiet, which becomes a knowing that it might not get perfectly quiet. I try the first line of "The Entertainer," the song I will perform soon for a competition. The second line. With my eyes closed. Then slower, to practice the switches. Faster, with my eyes closed. With eyes open, but looking out the window and not at the music. Slower, to make sure I learn which fingers curve how much and when and then when to stretch them out and up while switching positions and because I start to like the sound of the pads when they meet the metal, which is also how I practice not making a sound.

In fourth grade, I picked the flute as my instrument because a best friend picked it. I was afraid of picking the drums, the instrument (like the piano) I really wanted because I could play them and sing at the same time. Perspectival drawing might not be about space itself after all, but it does help think through choices not made: the further from a decision, the more space grows between where one set of consequences led and another might have. Each decision is a vanishing point, whole worlds fall away every time. But maps are hardly as precise as their lines, and I could spend a lifetime guessing which was an accident, and which was a decision, and how it matters to tease out distinctions when you're this far in.

At first my fingers on the flute were clumsy and heavy and confused. I practiced not because I liked to practice, but simply because I wanted it to feel different to hold it. Sometimes I practiced until it was time for dinner, even though it hurt to purse my mouth for hours. This is how I started loving the flute; this is how I started to think that work—to work—might not always lead only to exhaustion, might not be so bad after all, might not be building distance between me and everyone, might not only make me angry, might not make my chest boil, might not take more than it replenishes.

In the house where I practiced making fingers unclumsy, I watched *Xena: Warrior Princess* too many times on the leather couch, and some part of me started to believe in time travel and that I could become a knight's hostage amid the trees' dizzying limbs if I spun around fast enough. Which is why I only went into my forest a few days. Most other days I sat on the deck with my cousins when there were two pools and the two pools became the reason to pretend.

We were princesses because no one taught me yet that parts of my imagination could be something someone else called a cliché as though it was only embarrassing that so many of us watched racist Disney cartoons. It was over-determined that Belle with her books and Ariel with her singing would make the most sense to me. On Sundays I woke up earlier than I wanted to and sang in the church choir, waiting excitedly for the highest note in the descant, relaxing as I sustained it, floating in the air long enough for me to hear it get lost and smooth into other voices and instruments.

In all this I was curious about what was up with Xena, and thought there was something pretty great about the fact that, like She-Ra, she could fight anyone and win. And that she liked fighting. But with both, the problem was whether the metal bodice would fit over me, and that my imagination that could believe forests and lakes into being wasn't bold enough yet to dissolve the doubts.

With my cousins, I picked who would trek into the forest to see the wizard. Someone's kidnapped the king, and only the wizard knew where to look. The wizard had a potion to make us fly or to make us invisible to the guards. Sometimes it's my turn and it's like time travel and like getting lost, and I never entirely shake the sense that romance is going to feel that way even by the time I've learned to like feeling very still, in place, and firmly on the ground.

Other days, we are actresses in a dressing room on a set, and needing everything to be perfect, I order lemonade and tacos de lengua. Someone had to be the server and go into the kitchen. Abue knows we're playing a game, and plays along, bringing out the tacos on plates and serving them on the patio. ¡Ya están aquí sus taquitos, niñas!

We are Wilson Phillips in a music video, and we set up imaginary shots at the stairs of the pool: one of me, perched on the diving board singing—Just open your heart and your mind—then cut to my cousin walking along the fence: Mmm, Is it really fair to feel this way inside? I open the door of the guesthouse bathroom, and the camera meets me: Noooo.

I'm not close to the first migrants' kid to learn how to learn by watching television. Reruns. It's the way I still do it: by looking closely over and again, until I can start piecing together patterns where before there was just randomness and disconnection. It's comforting to review. I liked to test myself, to play the forgetting game—Hide and Keep—for the thrill of finding all the answers again. Meeting them the second time was not less fun than the first, and I wanted to know how many times that would last. I was not just nerdy but obsessive, and I looked for the cumulative review sections in textbooks first. It was like time traveling, where after became the place to begin and then return again. Someone else might have jumped rope, stayed longer on the swings, or made up a language with friends. I chose this game.

Donald in Mathmagic Land, Conan the Destroyer, Disney's Sword in the Stone, Purple Rain, The Making of "Thriller," The Care Bears Movie, The Smurfs and the Magic Flute, and Disney's Robin Hood. I recite these movies when I am trying to remember what I did when I was learning how to listen, which is learning how to watch, which is learning how to take the world in, how to play the flute and not make a sound at the same time. They are why I know to take Grace Jones seriously, why I know math and music are closer than they feel even if I don't spend that much time figuring out why, why the sense that hidden structures are part of where magic hides takes me back to and out of and back to graduate school, why I wanted to get green contact lenses despite having perfect vision in high school, why I think all love is stored in your gut and if only I can just beam it—and why I am sure it has to happen one day that a fox, an actual fox, will overthrow the illegitimate king of England. I unflinchingly trust the color blue and pigtails. After all, the most powerful beliefs are born not from anything "known," but from habits loved and unloved, the recognized ones, and the ones called by some other, some intelligible—by which I mean comfortable—name.

In fifth-grade biology, I started loving cumulus clouds because they were so low I thought I might touch them and because their edges were precise, which helped me tell the difference between the weather and the sky. But I also liked them because it didn't sound like English to aspirate the first consonant on the roof of my mouth: cumulus. Cumulative. Accumulate. A thick, if brief, stutter of sounds foreign to the smooth lines that otherwise make English efficient to look at and say, make English an easy battleground with which to demarcate.[1] Not as much power if the weapon arrived already loaded.

AUGUST 2002 *Cambridge, Massachusett homelands*
REVISED OCTOBER 2018 *Philadelphia, Lenni-Lenape homelands*

MAGICAL HABITS

2004

"BUENO, SÍ, MI'JA? Hola, mi'ja, buenas noches, cómo estás, how are you? That's good, real good. I'm glad I got you. Are you busy? Oh, that's good, then I won't keep you on the phone too long. You're still in school? Je je je, I know, I know. It just seems like a long time to me already. What do you want with so much school? What is there to know? You could probably teach all the classes. Of course you could! I've even taught classes! Sure I have, mi'ja. Here in Mexico they ask me all the time to come to the university to give classes, I don't know why, I don't know nothin', but just because of the restaurants, and the margarita, and the tequila, and now with the leasing companies. With all of that, they think I might know something. I don't know, maybe I do. But I don't know.

"Oh, about a year ago I taught a class on entrepreneurship. No, not the whole semester, just one time I went in and I told them, you know, you have to get focused. You have to choose. Before anyone teaches you anything, before you hear one word of what I am about to say, don't listen to anything I am saying without deciding: What do I want? It's so simple: *What* do *you* want? And most people, they just look at me when I ask them that question. I ask them, just like that, 'What do you want?' Don't laugh, I'm serious! They have their eyes blank, and just they're staring at me like someone should tell them what they want. It blows my mind! I'm telling you, it's unbelievable. Totally unbelievable. They don't know! Most people have no fuckin' idea what they want. So then they don't know what they want to do, because they don't have the reason, so they have no idea where to start because they have no idea where they are going or why they would want to do anything. They're outta their mind! It makes me so mad. Nothing makes me madder, I can't stand it. If I had half the brains that you had, or half the school! So I just do my little thing instead. Try to spend a few pesos here and there. At least I know what I want. ¡Ja!

"Right now, oh man, right now I'm in the middle of a big lawsuit. Oh, you study history, you might be interested. A year or two ago I was having a conversation with this family. And the family mentioned that they had these old bonds from the nineteenth century. You know who J. P. Morgan is, right? That's right, like the company. J. P. Morgan was one of the first bankers. Oh, you know that. Okay, so when the Mexican government was having financial problems in the nineteenth century—not so different from today, ¡ja ja ja! the Mexican government's always having a hard time—but during one really hard time, J. P. Morgan sold these bonds to the Mexican government, and he insured them. So that means that he backed them with his own money. Well, somehow, because of a war, or something, or someone died, who even knows why, but they got lost, passed down from one family to another in a bunch of unmarked boxes. And this family, who came to me one day, because now I had the leasing companies and they knew friends of mine, and they thought that I could help them, they showed them to me. I'll show them to you when you come. Are you coming? When are you coming? The summer? Oh, that's good, mi'ja, so when you come in the summer then I will show them to you. They are beautiful. I keep them in the safe at the house.

"They have these designs on them, even though they are technically just big checks. Anyway, they got lost, and no one ever claimed them. That's right, no one ever cashed them in. Until this family came and asked me for help. They wanted to know if they were worth anything. So I had a whole team of lawyers work on it for two or three years. Yeah, it took that long to do all the research, and make sure they were legitimate. 'Cause I don't know, what do I know about what nineteenth-century bonds look like, or this family could be nuts. We had to verify all the signatures that were a hundred and fifty years old! And get all the paperwork. That takes a long time.

"No, these aren't like the ones you use in the United States. These are Mexican archives. All it means is boxes of papers, no labels, no dates, no computer you can Google things. Boxes and papers. Random.

"Anyway, all this time, and all this work, and a ton of my money went into proving it, but we finally did it: they were real. We went before a judge, we had experts testify, the whole thing. They were authentic, the judge even said so. And I told the family that I would go and get their money—what do you mean from where? From J. P. Morgan. And I told them what percentage I wanted. We'd sunk—I had sunk all this money into the years and years and years of the process. And then they start fighting me for it. That it's theirs. That it's their family inheritance. All this bullshit. I said, listen, without the verification, they are just pieces of paper in your attic. *I* made them valuable, so I'm going to take a fee. And you're going to pay my expenses to go to New York and get the money.

"¡Ja ja ja! I went! Yes. I made an appointment, my assistant made it, and I flew to New York. Yes. Yes, mi'ja. Why would I be lying? Because I had sunk all this money into the project, so now I had a reason why I wanted them to pay up!

"I showed up at the offices of J. P. Morgan, with my briefcase. It was all I had, just the briefcase, copies of the court decisions, and a few of the bonds to show them, and that's it. I walked into the main building in the middle of Manhattan, I know, huge, huge building, and I was laughing to myself, thinking they have no idea. But I was also thinking, here I was, and who was I? I make tacos, and I'm going to convince them to listen to me and then to give me their money. For me, that was going to be more fun than stealing it.

"They took the meeting. ¡Ja ja ja!"

THE QUENE

A Mervilos and Magiquall Tale
of epistemological Mischief,
Wherein there are revealed no secretes

No tengo trono ni reina, ni nadie que me comprenda, pero sigo siendo el rey.
—JOSE ALFREDO JIMÉNEZ, "El Rey"

ot long ago and not far away, there lived a queen. Unlike other kingdoms whose
borders marked the difference between there and here, one side of her kingdom
a forest surrounded a deep blue lake; in the other half, a desert danced with the
wind. The border was inside.

The queen delighted in her divided kingdom and did not think there was a more
beautiful kingdom than her own. On clear days, she looked out from her throne, which
sat along the border between the desert and the forest, and thought, "How wonderful it
is to rule over such a kingdom as mine!"

The queen so loved her kingdom, half-forest, half-desert, that she never took off her
crown. Not in her bed—half red, half green. Not for her breakfast—half sweet, half sa-
vory. Not at lunch—half sandwiches, half cups of soup, half-full goblets of wine and half-
full pitchers of water. Not even when the sun went halfway down to make way for the
moon. She loved her crown because it, too, was unlike any crown she had ever seen. Like
her kingdom, her bed, her breakfast, and her lunch, it was split down the middle: half
gold and half silver. It hugged her forehead day and night, and when she walked toward
any room, it caught light first and brightly filled it, while the rest of her shape followed
in its gleam.

Being queen of a divided kingdom could have made the queen frustrated, or confused
about its nature. But, instead, having to balance the needs of the desert and the forest
had made the queen very fair-minded. She did not play favorites. Instead, each day she

would travel to the four corners of the kingdom to greet them each alike: "Hello, fair corner of my fair kingdom!" She would add a smile and a laugh and a twirl and a flourish—"I am the queen!" she would think with great pride—and then ride back to the castle, anticipated by the glow from her crown.

To protect both halves of her kingdom, the queen watched over a formidable army. And to help her rule, half her advisors and lieutenants came from the desert and half came from the forest. This way, and with great pleasure, the queen received advice that perfectly balanced the needs of her kingdom, and her advisors and lieutenants loved the queen dearly. They were very loyal to her, for she was generous and fair. On all matters they gave wise counsel, and nothing was more important to the queen than keeping her advisors happy and her kingdom peaceful.

But it happened often that the needs of the desert and the forest did not match, and that the advisors from the desert and the advisors from the forest disagreed, so different were even the daily concerns of desert and forest for provisions, for shelter, and for protection.

On one such day, Santiago, the head advisor from the desert, and Abel, from the forest, came to the queen in the midst of a deep disagreement.

"Santiago, you're being unreasonable. Every year the rains come, and every year the forest floods and our homes suffer damage. Would you have our stores depleted? We need to repair the aqueduct so water can be sent away from the kingdom."

"How can you say that to a man from the desert? We need to repair the aqueduct to bring more water toward the kingdom. All we need are better ways to store it once it gets here."

"Do you want the forest to flood?"

"Of course I don't want the forest to flood, Abel. But I can't imagine you want our people in the desert to go thirsty!"

Abel turned to the queen, who had been listening patiently to their conversation. "Your highness, this is where we are. It is like this every year when the rains come. What should be done?"

This time, as with all other times, when the needs of the two halves of the kingdom conflicted, there was no clear choice. Since the aqueduct ran through the forest, if the waters were brought to the kingdom the forest would flood. But if the aqueduct were directed away from the kingdom, it would be too far for the people of the desert. Even after so many years united under one sign, they could not help being distinct from one another, with distinct needs.

"I have heard you both, and I want to do what is best for the kingdom. What does the rest of the council say?"

"Their votes are evenly cast," replied Santiago.

"As with every vote, your highness," added Abel, whose temper had just then run thin.

"So it is," answered the queen, disregarding the frustration in Abel's voice. "Well, if the vote is split, there is only one thing to be done."

It happened with every deep conflict: as a response, the queen immediately announced that there was to be a party, and that the matter would be taken up again the next day.

The queen took pride in throwing lavish parties. The parties would be so grand, each whim of her advisors would be so deliciously met, that in the end no one would remember the dispute that had required throwing the party in the first place. The next day, advisors from the forest and the desert would again greet each other as intimate friends, no matter how sharp their exchanges had been, no matter the conflict that remained unresolved. Surely this time would be no different.

No less did her guests, half from the forest and half from the desert, enjoy the parties. Stewards offered drinks in half-gold, half-silver goblets, dancers and musicians performed unceasingly, mounds of roasted meats and wedges of cheese were heaped on tables next to thick slices of warm bread, and layered cakes gleamed with sugar glazes and buttercreams.

That evening, the queen found herself on a balcony, looking out on her kingdom. She could hear the brassy melody of her favorite song beginning, and it reminded her how satisfied, how full, how delighted she was throughout her days, how well she lived, how well she took care of her kingdom, her advisors, and her people. Everyone would have agreed, especially that night.

Just as the first guests were leaving, the queen withdrew to her chambers, passing the elaborate tapestries that lined the walls. One depicted her father's defeat of the army of invading horsemen. Another, her grandfather securing the peace between the desert and the forest. Her great-grandfather's face was calm in the third; he'd first united the desert and forest and established a lasting alliance with the sea merchants, who would ever after trade with the kingdom and bring goods from unknown empires. With each ruler the kingdom had grown more peaceful. It was for this reason that it only ever took a celebration to make the people forget their disagreements, so well had the old allegiances been forged, so beneficial to forest and desert alike. Compared to that which had come before, this was a time of bounty and of peace. The queen knew she was fortunate to be queen at this precise moment in the history of the kingdom.

That night she was in her preferred mood: serene and full of delight and deliciousness alike. Her advisors were once again merry and forgetful of worrisome aqueducts and potential droughts, of likely floods and the certainty that their needs would never match. Forgetful of all of that, the queen made her way to her half-red, half-green bed, and slept a sleep deep enough to forget even dreams . . .

A sliver of light opened the queen's eyes. At once the morning seemed to enclose her, and she thought her attendants must have left the curtains open just as she began to feel a startling tickle on her cheek. It took time for her to see through so much light. She raised her head and rubbed the prickly feeling from her cheek with her palm. The bedsheets, too, seemed altogether strange and very much like grass.

As her eyesight sharpened, a green square appeared beneath her. Indeed! It was a perfectly square patch of grass, fresh smelling, as though recently trimmed. The queen was not known for sleepwalking, but somehow she must have ended up outside the palace after the party.

Now that she could plainly see the grass, the queen looked up. Blinking once, twice, again, she looked around, but still the daylight was too sharp. She could not see anything: not her palace, not her grounds, not her fields of sheep, not the drawbridge, not the line of hitched horses her councilmen had ridden from desert and forest. There was only the green square on which she sat.

"Well, this is strange," the queen said to herself. "I must be dreaming. I will wake myself up." The queen lay back down. She had woken still in dreams before and knew exactly what there was to do. She stretched out on the grass with her arms by her sides and closed her eyes. She thought, "I am the queen, and the queen says, 'Wake up!'" Assuming her reliable trick had worked, she looked around only to find the same: a square patch of freshly-cut grass. "Well, this is strange."

The queen stood up, but, even standing, there was nothing in sight to see. She felt along the edge of the square patch of grass with her foot, wondering whither her foot might go if she stepped off. Oddly, her foot did not sink away, even when she pushed it down. Instead it hovered just at the height of the square patch of grass, no matter at which edge she pressed.

The queen reached out from the grass toward the sky, but met neither resistance nor breeze. The air she breathed was not hot and not cold and not medium and hardly felt like air at all. Her nightshirt was neither sufficient nor insufficient. The light must have been coming from somewhere unseen, but it did not vary, no matter where she looked.

It then occurred to the queen to check for her crown. She drew her hands to her forehead and grabbed at what was just her hair. Like her kingdom and everything in it, her crown had disappeared. She had never before appeared in her own dreams without her half-gold, half-silver crown.

"What is this dream then?"

The queen decided once again it was time to wake up. She sat on the grass, crossed her legs, and cradled her chin in her palm to wait for wakefulness. She began, simply, to count and so to pass the time. Perhaps this would also be a way to fall asleep to wake up.

As she counted, she noticed the light did not change or move or flicker. No shadows were cast in any direction. No matter how high she counted, the queen could not tell if time was really passing. And since she could not tell how much time had passed, the queen began to consider how that could be.

MAGICAL HABITS

It took practice. The queen had not troubled herself much before with considerations or curiosity. Her kingdom was peaceful and bountiful and no hunger or war had touched her people as long as she could remember. Her parties resolved any disagreements by inspiring all to forget discordance and to wake the next day once more in love with their queen.

For a long, long while, just in that way, the queen remained still and had no thoughts.

She reasoned into the unmoving atmosphere, "I am the queen! I rule over a kingdom that is half forest and half desert; surely I can do so simple a thing as wake up."

But there were no advisors to consult or to help her understand how it was her half-red, half-green bed, half-gold, half-silver crown, and half-desert, half-forest kingdom had disappeared in her sleep. In this bright quiet, the queen felt a feeling she could not name.

"But I am the queen! I am the queen and as the queen I command the thoughts to come!" She sat and waited for them to obey. She waited a bit. And then waited a bit more. But nothing changed and no thoughts came. There was only noiseless air and mysterious light, only the queen and her very new feeling.

"But I am the queen!" And, again, as soon as she had the thought, the queen could find no others.

"Well this is very *strange," she repeated and looked out into what there wasn't to see.*

She resolved that although she could not recognize the feeling she was having, she did know *the names of very many things. So instead of trying to think—which had not taken her very far—she recited the names she could name. She began, simply, with what she could remember about the previous night. She imagined her handsome guests sitting at long, wooden tables, the rows of fur-lined garments in her bedchamber, the number of times her scepter had knocked the stone floor as she walked from one entrance to her throne and back.*

Then her memory grew more specific. "Minced meat pies. Roast duck and roast pig. Lutes. Guitars. Dancers. Braided hair. Ladies' veils. Cornelius, the cook. Rebecca, the keeper of the palace. Laertes, the horse groom." Remembering Laertes reminded her of: "Brushes. Pelts. Shovels. Saddles," which reminded her of other things: "Table. Tree. Forest. Shade. Breath. Echo. Festivals. Ceremony. Gold. Amber. Honey. Honeybees. Wings. Tails. Fingernails." She let herself be led by the memories as much as by the memories' sounds when she made them into words.

In a moment, the queen stopped listing to listen for any thoughts that might have come with the names. She felt sure, "Now that I have remembered so many of the things I cannot see, they should arrive." But as soon as she stopped, there was only the soundless air and the square patch of grass. She preferred the noise of naming names to this steady, uncertain silence.

"I am the queen," she repeated, this time in a whisper. "The thoughts must come! Perhaps if I tell myself the stories I know of my father, grandfather, and great-grandfather, it will inspire thoughts of my own."

Her great-grandfather had not wanted to be king. Of the people who lived in the desert near the forest, he was like any other. He hunted what little there was to hunt, and made trade with the people from the forest for other provisions for his family. But he had one gift that no one else from either the desert or the forest had. He could read people. So great was his gift that, soon, people from both the desert and the forest would come to ask him whether someone was trustworthy. And the queen's great-grandfather, not thinking it special that he had this gift, would always answer honestly. None could come with bad intentions because they knew that he would read them at once.

The secret he never told anyone was that it was not reading at all. There was a tiny, faithful bird who would appear when someone was not a danger. If the bird stayed away, it was how he knew to be wary. But no tapestry included the tiny oracle, and so the kingdom was to always misremember what kept them safe was not their king alone.

The day the sea merchants found their way to the border between the forest and the desert—having walked over a hundred miles inland from the sea—it was the queen's great-grandfather who was called to speak with them on behalf of both the desert and the forest. Deeming the sea merchants trustworthy, the queen's great-grandfather encouraged the people from the desert and the forest to host them, even when some of the men were suspicious. "But we have heard tell of legends," said a few of them, "of men who come from the sea with bad intentions, who say they are searching for gold, but stay and take wives and homes and land instead."

"I have heard the same tales as you. And I had that fear as well. But I have talked with these men, and seen that these are not their intentions. They love their lives as sea merchants and have no interest in settling here. They want to trade with us for our animals, some of which they have never seen. They admire the wood carvings of the forest and the paintings of the desert. They want to bring these back to their lands, in exchange for what they have. We should host them, treat them well, and develop an alliance. I think we will all fare well if we do this."

He thought it was better for the bird to be a secret friend. He thought it would keep the bird's ways.

In this way, the queen's great-grandfather was proven right: through trading with the sea merchants the kingdom grew prosperous and more connected to other kingdoms. This was how the desert and the forest became one kingdom, united under the queen's great-grandfather, destined from then on to be two halves of a whole. Now that there was a union, and a reason to grow stronger, each could give the other of its wisdom. The kingdom flourished, its people knew peace, and one half became the kingdom's proud symbol. Through its repetition the desert would always think of the forest, and the forest would always remember the desert. And no one would remember the bird.

After growing prosperous befriending other kingdoms, it was only a matter of time before conflict befell the kingdom. It was the queen's father who faced the dreaded army of skilled horsemen from the south. Since there had been no route connecting the forest and desert to the sea prior to trading with the merchants, the army of horsemen had stayed away; they had simply not known about the kingdom. As soon as the horsemen heard that a kingdom was prospering to the north, they sent spies. Along the road, the spies heard stories about the queen's father, who was now king, a strong and beloved leader, who inherited his father's wisdom, and who had the humility to learn from his advisors as well. Because the queen's father, like his grandfather before him, was so beloved, the general of the army of horsemen decided that there would be no way to infiltrate the kingdom. He planned a surprise attack instead.

Early on the morning of the attack, one of the king's foragers, who happened to be at the outskirts of the forest, caught sight of one section of the horsemen army's encampment. Immediately, he ran to tell the king. The king had the loyalty of this forager to thank for having time to ready his mighty army for battle. After the victory, the king handsomely rewarded the forager, and made him a trusted advisor. In this way the king showed that he valued loyalty and made all his people proud.

The queen's father, then, ruled over a kingdom that had grown prosperous, and whose victory over the horsemen army helped secure neighboring kingdoms' respect. The queen's father, having little unrest or conflict thereafter in his kingdom, maintained good relations with the sea merchants and all neighboring kingdoms. In this way, and for this reason, the kingdom maintained the peace and grew wealthier still.

The queen, then, became a woman in a time of bounty, with no turmoil, many friendly neighbors, frequent visitors from foreign lands, and countless celebrations. She was cheerful as a little girl, surrounded by so many reasons for being cheerful. She loved and respected her father and aimed to mirror him in every way. This was how she learned to be queen. When her father died, she honored his death by continuing to imitate him. Although she would not be blessed with the deep intuition or wisdom of her great-grandfather, the queen herself was studious and meticulous in all her affairs.

These stories the queen retold herself just as she had heard and recited them at festivals, as they had been sung by musicians, echoing through hallways made of stone, depicted on the tapestries she walked past each night. These stories were dear to her and made her homesick.

She had come to the end of what she could name and remember. There were no more stories she knew to tell. These were all the thoughts she knew how to have, but had found neither comfort nor a solution to the square patch of grass, the undetectable light, and the unpassing of time. "But I am the queen!," she said again with more frustration than she knew she could feel. "I am the queen! More thoughts must come. I command them! I am the queen!"

And at that moment, the queen remembered one more memory and knew exactly what there was to do: there would be a party.

As best she could, she performed the rituals: She made the square patch of grass ready by brushing the blades until fresh seeming. She straightened her nightshirt. She imagined platters of shiny cakes, roasted pork bellies and braised short ribs, goblets of wine, piles of warm bread piled up. She made believe the dancers were waving streamers just beyond, over there, and that the musicians were at the ready to play the only song she knew by heart as she entered the great hall. She heard the trumpets and let the bright glow of her half-gold, half-silver crown that was not on her head surround her and fill the space. She looked out beyond the square patch just as she had looked out over her kingdom.

She started singing as though casting a spell, "I don't have a throne, a crown, an army, or a kingdom, but I am the queen!"

Just there, on a square patch of grass lit from an unknown source, where there is no weather, no time, and no room for confusion, the queen lives well—sleeping when tired, dancing when merry, turning now, turning then, to each corner of a green square to announce herself to herself, to no one, and to the still air. And whenever the queen feels otherwise, she simply throws herself a party and sings her favorite song.

7. before and after

You take in things you don't want all the time. The second you hear or see some ordinary moment, all its intended targets, all the meanings behind the retreating seconds, as far as you are able to see, come into focus. Hold up, did you just hear, did you just say, did you just see, did you just do that? Then the voice in your head silently tells you to take your foot off your throat because just getting along shouldn't be an ambition.—CLAUDIA RANKINE, *Citizen: An American Lyric*

A PHOTOGRAPH IS LIKE A POEM: it betrays its limits by announcing that it is the limit (just a square, just some shapes and shadows, just the fictional, even literary, appearance of a day in an instant of light, a generation) and then enchants us anyway.[1] I looked at the pictures for a long time, and kept hoping the story they had to tell would change, like a broken spell casting a new one. The waves of belief are waves in that they can wash over you and soak in even when they are unclung to.

I kept all the pictures of my dad in a notebook to lose and forget, so that I could rediscover them on a day I couldn't predict, know that I had kept them to lose, and feel all the time in between, when I'd forgotten they were there. There could only be so many faces in the house at once, and if his wasn't one of those, what good use did photographs have? They'd found their way into a box I packed up for college. When the photographs reappeared in my dorm room and I decided to look (I could have put them away again), they asked me to look in a mirror, the way an avatar might speak to you.[2] It was grudgingly and with some anger that I noticed the pattern called resemblance.[3]

In one, my sister tugs at the loose flesh on his neck while making turkey noises, even though it wasn't Thanksgiving, even though we were in public, even though other people could hear, even though we were in Europe. When he turned to look at things, it was a second body sitting on his chest. It also turned to look. I couldn't guess what was in there, but I decided it was either another life or sounds that got caught. If it had been mine, I would have hidden all my wishes there, as if it were the wilderness in a fairy tale, so that I could rescue them and afterward return home to a cheery burst of golden trumpets.

The fairy tale is the certainty of an end, and a beginning, and the romance that a certainty like that can be pressed out from a living that's filled with much more quiet, and mist, and twilight. Particles. The fairy tale is the comfort of form, of the finite infinity implied by happily ever afters.

The first time he shaved off his mustache I was nine. It was my sister's quinceañera, and he wore a tuxedo. He had shrunk by two hundred and fifty pounds. I overheard that part, but what I already knew was that he was a different shape. His cheeks drooped above the tuxedo; he looked taller, and more serious, processing down the aisle out of the church with my sister while the mariachi played "Guadalajara" and by the time they got to the part where Guadalajara tasted like wet dirt, my grandmother cried and smiled at the same time. My grandmother made the dresses we were both wearing, and I tried to like the lace on mine, the pink ribbon around where my waist should have been, the flower corsage my mom pinned on me, the French braid, the teased and curled 1980s bangs in the fall of 1990.

The party and the rest of the ceremony were in the ballroom of the Marriot in Oak Brook. He whisked my sister across the floor of the ballroom to "The Blue Danube," then danced with my mother—who hardly looked at him—to "Everybody, Everybody." The DJ started playing the Black Box song when it was his turn to turn the end of dessert into a dance party for my sister's high school friends and the "business friends" he wanted to impress with a two-hundred-person party.

He had changed shape since the turkey picture, and his voice might have changed pitch too. I noticed during his speech before "Everybody, Everybody." In choir, I learned a person can manipulate how sounds come out beyond the volume, can affect the shape, the brightness, the height. I wasn't sure yet which parts to hold tight, or how to control volume without seeming to, to make it easier for those listening to only pay attention to how the sounds made them feel, the way part of the work of craft is to become something else, to make something other and else. I liked the word *shape* only when it became a verb I could do much later. He thanked the guests for coming, he wished my sister a happy birthday with his new voice coming from his new shape. My mom's bangs bounced as she walked up to meet him, and they were fluffy, and all three of ours matched. He invited "everybody everybody" to the dance floor, and I was embarrassed he made the joke.

My cheeks got red quickly from dancing in white tights. I still cannot do the Roger Rabbit or the Running Man. I found a place to nap with all the coats because no one was as ready as I was to go home, so there was no point in asking.

Two decades later, I watched the video from that night with my mom. Neither one of us spent that morning fluffing bangs, so a part of me started to believe, faintly, in progress. The video, I thought, could help me see whether resemblances fade. She'd brought it with her because I asked her to. Ay, para qué quieres eso, Mónica? Just to watch it, I said, as though that were a benign sort of thing to do.

When sleeping next to my mom, I liked to wrap my legs close around hers. I liked to press my back against her stomach, soft and warm, somehow spacious, somehow loose, how I thought (incorrectly) all mothers' stomachs must be—as proof. Around her stomach, the skin accordioned with stretch marks and rested in what looked like whispers I thought I could hear against the tops of her thighs. It looked frayed sometimes, that skin, and other times like work, like the strenuous work of echo. I pressed back into it, and there was space for me. I liked her arms around me and her breath on my hair. I thought my skin would never be that soft and I asked her why. Ay, Mónica. Ponte cremita. Síguete poniendo cremita y ya verás. Your skin will get soft. I wondered whether first I needed a stomach as proof before I earned skin that soft, whether there were other ways of being soft, whether each time we had to figure out what it meant to be a mother, and to be a child, unfolding into one another as into time.

She moved back to Chicago from Boca Raton because she hadn't been able to manage the last restaurant alone from that far away. In Naperville, she likes open spaces and finds the suburban cornfields comforting. The year before I found my way onto her stomach to replay my sister's quinceañera, the last restaurant closed. She had flown in from Naperville to see me. Like many graduate students I lived in a basement studio in Oakland, when Oakland was still a place where a graduate student could afford to live. The door opened out onto a shady garden and patio that Susan had been working on her whole life.

Susan and Stephanie owned Susan's childhood home. My Bay Area Moms, I called them, even after I moved back to the East Coast. At the Craigslist "interview," she beamed when I said I was doing a PhD in the English Department at Cal. (Two years into the program, I'd learned to call it Cal as though that were the only thing it could be called.) Stephanie loved that I studied literature. But I'm really interested in photographs, I said apologetically. How are you with dogs? Because sometimes we'll let Annie out. We want for you to feel like this is your home; let us know if she bothers you, and we won't let her out while you are outside.

She said she stayed near Chicago so that my little brother didn't have to switch schools the way I did at his age. When David finishes high school, she said, maybe I'll move to California. By then, I answer, I won't be here anymore. She laughed. She didn't leave Naperville when David started at DePaul. I lived in Jersey again, but had stopped back in Brooklyn, with two years in Durham in between. Last June, David graduated from DePaul in a virtual ceremony I watched from Philadelphia. She still lives in Naperville, but maybe not for long.

While I fast-forwarded past photomontages that the quinceañera video man spliced between dancing guests, I asked, What were you thinking while you two were dancing? She said something too lonely-sounding to repeat, not because she wanted to depress me, just that some words aren't said when they are truest but manage to preserve their sting. Plus, she didn't know her words were that strong. Honesty can have different pitches, but she didn't sing in choir so it's possible she doesn't know how to both change tone and maintain the sound. Or, there was a mistranslation. At least your dress was great. Do you still have it? I don't know, it might be somewhere; I've given away so much, or maybe in storage. Maybe the most Mexican thing about us is not how much we've moved, but how scattered our archives are.

A professor told me once: What you think is essential to who you are, one day it's no longer going to be true, and the person you call yourself may be some-

MAGICAL HABITS

one completely different. Does it stop? I asked. No, he laughed at me because he had great affection for my impatience, but he also thought it was silly. He added, It just keeps on happening. This was his version of comfort.

The most obvious thing is, like my mom, I left clothes behind: turtlenecks stayed in Burr Ridge, sweater-vests and polo shirts for high school and bell-bottom jeans for Fort Lauderdale's clubs stayed in Boca Raton, empire-waist dresses for the late summers in Oakland. I've given away so much clothing there are hundreds of people all over the country who dress like all the versions of me I dreamed up and now forget and keep for when I want to review them all.

But there was also the *me* of two lines of handwriting squeezed into one line of loose-leaf paper, taking detailed notes on Mesopotamia for a high school ancient history exam, the pleasure of squeezing one more detail onto a line, the *me* who figured out in the meantime I needed to write it down to remember; the recording secretary *me* who too enthusiastically welcomed first-years and newcomers to the Kuumba Singers of Harvard College; the *me* interested in a martini, a gin and tonic, a Jack and ginger, who chose a different drink for every season; the *me* of pulses taken by an acupuncturist in Berkeley once a week for years; the *me* on monthly trips to the Container Store to wander in all that order, hoping to memorize it; the *me* who tried very hard (and failed) to enjoy reading the *New Yorker* straight through; the *me* who let that dream go and accepted that what I wanted to look at when I wasn't work-reading wasn't wry comics that were never either funny or charming and critical commentary (so much of which studiously—which is to say for politeness' sake—avoided feeling responsible for a suffering world) but cat memes and videos of baby animals or webcams aimed at red pandas; the *me* doggedly chasing a solution for history; the *me* grudgingly accepting history doesn't go anywhere but it can be reviewed and you can find a spot from which to turn on a heel, exhaling ancient breath, letting its hold go (a hold that grasps together all the logics of disconnection), even as you know, like a cumulative review, in an instant, the instant of a pulse, it could return. What else but to turn until your heels wear thin? It could be like dancing. But there was also the *me* of detecting with a telescope instead of a magnifying glass, ready to decipher imprints on the moon or on people across long stretches not always of space but of time.

Before his Food Network television show, and before his brands of salsa arrived in your local grocery store aisles, Rick Bayless made Mexican restaurants acceptable as fine dining in Chicago. In 1987, Bayless opened Frontera Grill, his first Mexican restaurant, to immediate praise.[4] Even as Bayless might wince at the comparison, as a non-Mexican who gains success and renown through selling Mexican food, his most obvious predecessor is Glen Bell, the founder of Taco Bell, who opened his first taco stands in mid-twentieth-century California. Originally from Kansas, Bayless's success was made possible, in part, by the growing popularity of Mexican restaurants in the late 1980s and 1990s.

Born in Oklahoma City to a white American family of barbecue restaurateurs, Bayless's claims to authenticity could not come from his own ethnic background. In his menu there are no family biographies, no family portraits, no immigration narratives, and no translations for the food.[5] Instead, in interviews he stresses his research; he emphasizes that he learns how to make authentic Mexican food from authentic Mexicans. One way that the Frontera Grill menu creates its sense of Mexicanness is through using the Spanish names of ingredients. Mexicanness, for him, is an intellectual project, not a relation verified through family histories of migration and displacement.[6] Chile pasilla, chile guajillo, and jícama appear more frequently on Bayless's menu than on either Nuevo León's or Salvador's, even as they were common ingredients in both.

Critics do not refer to *his* authentic Mexican food but, rather, to "authentic contemporary regional Mexican" food. The implications are twofold. First, it is implied that other Mexican food is not "contemporary" but somehow from the past. Secondly, it suggests that Bayless's food is a revision of "ordinary" Mexican food; his revision belongs to the "contemporary" moment. At the same time, his emphasis on having learned Mexicanness in Mexico continues to situate some ineffable thing about authenticity in Mexico, even as the food, through the fact of his unremarked ethnicity and biography, can become contemporary. Phil Vettel, the head food critic at the time for the *Chicago Tribune*, praises Frontera Grill and Topolobampo as "no ordinary Mexican restaurant[s]."[7] However, instead of criticizing Bayless's food for being inauthentic, Vettel celebrates it: "Dining here is worth whatever effort is required," because it is "Mexican food at its finest."[8] Vettel might be referring by contrast to the "home-style" Mexican food that Gutiérrez and Huerta serve in their restaurants. But, since he is not Mexican, Bayless is not understood through the models of ascribing authenticity that surveil Gutiérrez and Huerta. Bayless, therefore, uses Mexicanness as a source of cultural capital at the same time that the restaurants and the food are free from the constraints of being authentic in a prescribed way. Food critics have heralded his takes as "Mexican food at its best." Bayless is given license to reinvent the terms of authenticity through which he is evaluated and to which he can lay claim.

Even if Bayless himself does not have to answer the same kinds of questions as other restaurant owners, nor perform his domestic life in public as part of the same, he typically employs chefs of Mexican descent. It was in Bayless's Frontera Grill kitchen, for example, that Geno Bahena began to brainstorm his own restaurants. Bahena worked in Bayless's restaurants for a combined twelve years. He was at Frontera Grill from its inception, and he eventually became managing chef at Topolobampo. In several instances, he is credited in Bayless's cookbooks.[9]

With training in Mexican cooking from both Joliet Junior College and from Bayless, Bahena opened his first restaurant, Ixcapuzalco, in 1995.[10] Bahena, like Bayless, emphasizes his culinary research in the thirty-one states and capital of Mexico.[11] Yet unlike Bayless's account of knowledge through research, the Ixcapuzalco menu reverts to biography: "Growing up and working on his family's ranch and orchard, Bahena explains that he developed a respect for the things of the earth. He was able to see how hard work and dedication transform raw ingredients into high quality foodstuffs."[12] Just like Huerta's and Gutiérrez's stories, this one uses an ethic of hard work to justify Bahena's success. While Chicago is the primary setting, the story describes Mexico as Bahena's "native" land and the source of his knowledge about Mexican food.

In the Ixcapuzalco menu, Bahena's personal history is presented as "the foundation upon which Geno's passion and love for the food of his native Mexico has grown."[13] His "passion and love," rather than his research, endow the food with authenticity. Bahena strives to "preserv[e] his family traditions," despite "Geno and his cooking [being] described as adventurous and creative, but most of all, passionate."[14] The story in his menu positions "preserving family traditions" in opposition to Bahena's "creativity" and "adventurous" cooking. This opposition carries at least two different meanings. First, even though Bahena spent twelve years working for Bayless, it is his family's ranch that serves as the foundation of his knowledge of Mexican food in the story. Second, Bahena strives to differentiate his food through emphasizing "creativity" and "adventure." The menu presents him not as a skillful expert but as a dutiful son who is carrying forth his family's values and kitchen secrets into the American marketplace.

Yet, working at Frontera Grill and Topolobampo for twelve years influenced Bahena's cooking. Bahena's restaurants were often referred to in relation to

Bayless's because of their previous connection. But it is specifically Bayless's innovation that is said to have influenced Bahena's restaurants. The headline of a *Tribune* review from 2000 proclaims, "Former Topolobampo Chef Geno Bahena Hits a Home Run."[15] In this review, Vettel here lauds Bahena's second restaurant, Chilpancingo, by comparing his food to Bayless's, who by then had already become a marker of what distinguished Mexican food as superior.[16] Vettel, for example, does not give Bahena equal credit for influencing Bayless. Instead, Bahena's inclusion in Bayless's cookbooks bestows culinary authority on Bahena. Bayless's role as restaurateur relies on his expertise, his skill, his mastery, and his vision. In other words, where Bayless's contemporary Mexican food proves a kind of expertise that can be thought as separate from his identity, for Bahena, his skills and creativity can be thought only as enactments of his Mexicanness, even as his food needs the relation with Bayless to be worthy of critical attention.

⟶

The habit of dancing between after and before means, in part, that I was waiting for time to feel real, even if time is an imperfect way to measure and the means by which we measure it are always in question (days? weeks? seasons? grad school? generations?): upon mastering one rule, it's easy to discover a reason it could be incomplete. Beginnings slip backward like endings vanish into another day. My very first impulse was to make things disappear in boxes, in cities where I no longer lived, in the unromance of the garbage. How else could I believe a day passed if any of yesterday stuck around? From Boca Raton I headed to Massachusetts for college (nothing like New England to best shatter the imagination of pink Spanish revival strip malls and palm trees strung with twinkle lights), then to Jersey for first graduate school, then Manhattan for martinis, to a cozy nook in Clinton Hill, then to Guadalajara and back to Manhattan, hoping all the while to outpace history.

From there, as I was trying to become an academic, a scholar, a professor, a person who finds fissures and patterns and architecture and ambivalence and alternatives for alternatives that have worn thin, I followed training and jobs and desire to Berkeley and Oakland just as the global economy crumbled, and to Albuquerque briefly before returning to Oakland and bouncing back, it now seems inevitably, to Cobble Hill, where I stayed in a friend's apartment and then, after a few months, to Crown Heights. Those twins, settler colonialism and racial capitalism, destroy in cycles and waves so that it's easy to mistake either as seasonal shifts, except that they have both ever been fighting the weather and making the weather and my restlessness as I surfed the conjoined economy that produced and produces institutions of higher education into yet another of their weapons.

That was the last time I lived in New York, and after two years in Durham, two more in Jersey, I live in Philadelphia. I played geography hopscotch to lose and find days, believing fiercely in the magic of Elsewhere. Some of those moves, I chose and I could choose them because I had some bits of family money. Some of those moves were also about money, but the way money has shaped the shape of being an academic. Many of those moves cost more money than I had to pay, so I spent away savings and gathered up debt instead.

But I kept moving cities, in part, because timelines and clocks—like maps— play tricks on us. That is, I was hoping to be tricked. It's an act like faith to believe in a minute that lasts sixty seconds. How does it work to divide infinity, how does it work to believe in clocks as though it didn't happen that at some point someone had to start it? And really there's no use in getting worked up by the math after that, whether you're in Oakland or Brooklyn. Day and night are constant, and beyond that, no one keeps track of your time but you, even when you tether it to and make sense of it with the news, with the train schedule. The jobs that keep track of your time work not through keeping track of time but through taking time over to be Time.

Maybe what Time needs is time to settle down and coat me over like paint instead of trailing behind me like crumbs I've been leaving for whom but me to find? If there's no way off a map, if we've drawn all of them (we haven't— where's the map that connects me to you to everything?), and drawn ourselves into them with no blank spaces, only borders, what's the point in finding new points that are only new to me? More than a map, we might need a poem, a source of disorientation to find the stars anew, which is to say to be them.

That didn't count, I said when I didn't want to count one of them as an ex-boyfriend. A friend chides, You don't think anything counts! No, it can count a little bit, but what if I don't need it to count *all the time*? What if there are perfectly fine ways of living without remembering that one part one time? Why do we have to remember everything all the time? But in the meanwhile, for when I might need it, I need somewhere to put it.

Some people build mansions and museums for theirs, but to keep for later I hid the memories I didn't need in Lake Michigan, in the wide-open face that stays too calm to be an ocean, frozen cloudy in the long winters and dotted with friendly sailboats all at once with the first hints of spring and summer. I renamed it El Lago del Olvido because oblivion is a place too, and like any place, we get lonely on its behalf if we don't give it a name, when we don't give it space on our maps.

APRIL 2001 *Cambridge, Massachusett homelands*
REVISED DECEMBER 2017 *Princeton, Lenni-Lenape homelands*

"Skip this restaurant—food and service is lousy, place is dirty"—JTGraziano

First of all, I love mexican food and eat it any chance I can get. My girlfriend and I went to Barro Mexican Restaurant on my birthday on a Saturday evening and our experience was so bad we decided to pay up and leave after having our appetizers. For starters, the waiter took 15 minutes to show up with the menu and to take our drink order. During this time we had time to look around at the dirty walls, floor and fixtures. We each ordered an appetizer—mine was a tortilla soup in a chicken broth with a chunk of guacamole, a chunk of onion and glob of cheese floating in it. Looked gross and tasted terrible. I ate better food as a broke college student on a buzz at 2 AM. The fish in the ceviche I ordered was non-existent; instead the onions, tomatoes, cilantro and lime juice were abundant. The ceviche was served with musty smelling corn chips. . . . My girlfriends' empanadas were cold right out of the kitchen. For $26.00 we had 3 lousy appetizers and I had a Negro Modelo. And get this . . . after the cashier asked me how the meal was, I told him it was terrible at which point he told me he didn't want to hear about the complaint because he was working there that night on his birthday as a favor and really didn't want to take a complaint. Guess he shouldn't have asked. Needless to say, we won't be coming back.

BY: Mike P.

I can't believe I haven't reviewed Salvador's yet.

Ladies and Gentlemen of Chicago Yelp, Salvador's is the best Mexican Restaurant in Chicagoland. Huge menu, awesome margaritas, and good prices. It cannot be beat. The Mayan Palace comes close, but not quite. The North Avenue location is the second location for the place. It was originally at Lake and Ridgeland in Oak Park, across the street from the guitar store.

Order the margarita on the rocks, please. If you want a frozen drink, get a Slurpee at 7-Elevens.

November 10, 2006

"Is a burrito a sandwich?

"The Panera Bread Co. bakery-and-café chain says yes. But a judge says no, ruling against Panera in its bid to prevent a Mexican restaurant from moving into the same shopping mall.

"Panera has a clause in its lease that prevents the White City Shopping Center in Shrewsbury from renting to another sandwich shop. Panera tried to invoke that clause to stop the opening of an Qdoba Mexican Grill.

"But Superior Court Judge Jeffrey Locke cited Webster's Dictionary as well as testimony from a chef and a former high-ranking federal agriculture official in ruling that Qdoba's burritos and other offerings are not sandwiches.

"The difference, the judge ruled, comes down to two slices of bread versus one tortilla.

"'A sandwich is not commonly understood to include burritos, tacos and quesadillas, which are typically made with a single tortilla and stuffed with a choice filling of meat, rice, and beans,' Locke wrote in a decision released last week.

"In court papers, Panera, a St. Louis–based chain of more than 900 cafes, argued for a broad definition of a sandwich, saying that a flour tortilla is bread and that a food product with bread and a filling is a sandwich.

"Qdoba, owned by San Diego–based Jack in the Box Inc., called food experts to testify on its behalf.

"Among them was Cambridge chef Chris Schlesinger, who said in an affidavit: 'I know of no chef or culinary historian who would call a burrito a sandwich. Indeed, the notion would be absurd to any credible chef or culinary historian.'"

2006

"NO, THE GREEN IGUANA flavor wasn't first. First, we did Señorita Strawberry. But before that we were the first in the entire liquor business to find
a way to put tequila in the margarita and sell it. Because remember, before
Salvador's came out, no one was selling margarita; everyone was selling margarita mix—Cuervo, Sauza, did Bacardi have theirs then? I can't remember.
You had to buy the tequila separately. Sure! You don't know how long I had to
fight to make that happen. They thought I was crazy at first because no one
had ever done it before. Oh, man. But that's not even the first thing we didn't
agree about. First was the name for the margarita.

"It was so funny: they had done this focus group to see what name would
sell the most margarita. I don't know who they had in the room, I don't know
who they paid to ask questions, I don't know what kind of questions they
asked, they didn't ask me for any suggestions and I thought that was crazy—I
had been selling margaritas for twenty years![1] If they would have asked me,
I woulda told them the only name was gonna be Salvador's. Just Salvador's.
That was my name, so that was going to be the name for my margarita. Simple. But they came back, and you shoulda seen 'em, they were so proud of
themselves! They came back and had a whole presentation in front of the
president of Hiram Walker, and the board, they had a PowerPoint, they had
music, they had a slogan.[2] What was it? I think it was 'Start a fiesta with Hector's!' I know, it's terrible. I started laughing in the meeting 'cause I couldn't
fuckin' believe it! They were getting all this money, and spending all this time
to come up with *Hector's*! Who the hell was Hector?

"Right. I didn't have a presentation—I still don't know how to use a computer!—I didn't have a focus group, but I had a slogan and I made them put it everywhere: 'Tequila's in it!' What could be more Mexican than that? And more American than that? ¡Ja! People loved it. The name was harder, that took a few more meetings. But I told them that was the only way we were goin' ahead with it. If they didn't like my name or if their focus groups wanted to drink what Hector gave them, I would take my recipe and my idea and my slogan somewhere else. Without me, they had nothin'.

"The recipe I really did make in the restaurants over a long time. There's a million bad ways to make a margarita, you know.

"Hiram Walker was the biggest and most important, but there were other liquor distributors in the United States, and I even threatened to go to their main competitor. I knew somethin' they didn't know I knew: the presidents of both companies hated each other. I think one of them slept with the other one's wife or something. ¡Ja! No, I'm kidding, I don't know that. Something, but they hated each other. So once I said just the name of the other company, the president of Hiram Walker panicked and signed off on it. That's when the real fun started. Aw, man!

"So first we just came out with the traditional flavor: Salvador's World Famous Margarita. I started traveling, going to expos, to festivals, to television stations, to car shows. It didn't matter: they sent me everywhere. By that point we all knew I was going to be the reason this thing worked, so I got on planes and worked. It was nuts! I hardly slept.

"When we did the Señorita Strawberry launch, we were having this big event at the Alamo. It was the celebration for the anniversary of the Alamo, and there were thousands of people there. They took us around to look at the grounds, so that we knew where the Salvador's tent was going to be. That's when I saw the fountain. Have you ever been there? Right, so the fountain is right in front, made out of stone, it's beautiful. I saw it and said, 'We gotta fill that with margarita, and let people drink out of it with straws.' 'You wanna do what?' the supervisor asked me. ¡Ja! 'I want people to be able to drink margarita out of the fountain.' He said, 'That's not going to happen.' But guess what, that night I was handing out straws, and watching people kneel next to the fountain. They thought I was crazy, but then I saw the supervisor doing it too! Hundreds of people drank out of the fountain. We had to keep filling it!

"Then when Green Iguana came out, oh man, you'll never believe what I did! It was spring break, I think it was Tampa Bay, or New Orleans. One of those big spring break places with all the college kids. So, first, I had thousands of glow-in-the-dark condoms made. No, not just green, in the shape of an iguana! That's right! They loved it. But that wasn't enough, so we went around with the girls—oh, the girls, yeah, my oldest daughter managed them for a while. No wait, I don't think she was doing it then. No, she wasn't. It was too early. Well, we had the girls go around and hand them out, but we had to get the kids to come to the tent at night, you know, we were having a big party to promote the margarita. So we told them, if you come wearing these, you'll get in for free! Cover was, I don't know, ten dollars, fifteen dollars, something like that, and you could drink free margarita all night, so obviously these kids were going to wear them. Some of the girls were even coming in wearing the glow-in-the-dark condoms around their necks, like necklaces, and on their hands! I'm serious!

"But *that* wasn't enough. So the last part was that I wanted to make a shot, a special shot for the night, using Green Iguana, but I wanted to use the condoms. Hiram Walker loved me by this point, but they also thought I was completely nuts for what I was willing to do. They thought I was insane, but at the same time they were making a lot of money, so they didn't really want to stop me, but they wanted to cover their ass.

"So I had these condoms, and I wanted to make a shot. I spent most of the day—while the girls were handing out condoms—figuring out what I wanted the shot to be like, and how we were going to use all these condoms. I was thinking, should we have a Big Iguana contest? ¡Ja ja! Or should we have contests where we fill them with water and have a Big Boobs contest, to see which boobs could carry the water-filled thing across the stage without dropping it—I don't know, I was thinking all kinds of things.

"And then, I remembered that shot, the Blow Job. But I wanted to do something better. So we made a shot with Green Iguana and Cointreau, and used seltzer water, and a little bit of baking soda—yeah, baking soda. But wait—we covered the shot glass with the iguana condoms, and then shook it until it fizzed! That was the shot! That was how we were going to use up all the extra condoms!

"Are you kidding me? The kids went nuts."

c. 1992

Author's personal collection

Promotional display for Salvador's Margarita

c. 1992
Author's personal collection

8. when courts of love have cash registers

And neither world thought the other world's thought, save with a vague unrest. — W. E. B. DU BOIS, "Of the Coming of John"

ON A DECEMBER MORNING in a Chicago courtroom, he walked to the defendant's table from the opposite side of the room as my mom. She kept her head down until she reached the table where the plaintiff sits. I read the angle his nose made in the air as the word *intrepid*, but was no less confused because I could name it. Thrown over her handcuffs, she had her fur coat. It was the coat she wore to church on Sundays; she would not wear it to church on Sundays the years when she did not go to church. In the winters of Chicago, she would wear it when she moved back from Florida and started hosting prayer circles and attending religious retreats. That's when she went to church on Sundays again. She eventually gave the coat away, because someone else might need it more than she did. He did not have a fur coat to throw over his handcuffs. Her nose was not intrepid. And a part of me wondered if they were in the same room.

The previous afternoon, his angry teeth had sunk into her next husband's hand, finger, and cheek. At some point it's not anger anymore and it's the need to destroy or be destroyed. Anger is a strenuous teacher. The teeth would not let go, even after blood ran, blood that he may not have tasted. My mom jumped on his back to try to pull them apart. At the hospital, there were rabies shots, my mom had told us from behind the thick glass partition at the police station the night before. The curve on her lips folded wryly as she said, simply, Imagínate, as though my sister or I might want to. Years later, when he tells me the story (as though I hadn't been there in the aftermath), he throws his head back and laughs so I see his teeth.

The chair I am sitting in is uncomfortable, and it feels like the chairs in middle school, when I waited inside to get picked up from school because it was too cold outside and she was late again. I try to pay attention to what she is saying behind the glass, but all I see is the thick plate, how it is smudged with fingerprints, how it seems too concentrated to be glass, and when I knock on it with curious knuckles, it doesn't sound like glass. My sister is holding the phone that goes nowhere, to just beyond our faces, to her ear.

The next day, he smiled at me in the clerical office, on the first floor below the courtroom, after they were both released on bail. What kind of smile and was it intrepid? Their open divorce case in Florida gave the judge a reason to let them go. But it seems like a strange fiction that Florida is far enough away from Chicago to make a difference, to make one judge succumb to another.

I see his new girlfriend and do not think of the word *girlfriend*, because even correct words can feel inappropriate. She has long hair like my mother did in the portrait my grandma kept in the closet in the house in Guadalajara where she lived for half the year until she couldn't be safe alone anymore. It was across the street from the park where I drank my first beer, where I made friends with the neighborhood boys who played soccer there. In the portrait, my mother's hair is straight and black and shiny and down to her waist. I'd heard Tía Celia and my grandma talk about her long hair at Christmases, and during all the summers in Guadalajara. Her black dress flirts with the tops of her thighs. I search for a pair of shorts or a skirt underneath what has no underneath. They are standing next to each other and already seem like adults to me, even with fresh skin, when her teeth were still crooked, when leather blazers and fringe were everyone's good idea.

Someone pulled it out from the closet when all four of us sat on the bed together, after everyone cried, after ultimatums, and after heartfelt, teary promises I must have believed before I believed something else. She seemed convinced. This was not long before we're in a courtroom in Chicago and I'm watching noses, keeping track of teeth and the cash register.

Her faith—if it was faith—gave out quietly.

⟿

I don't know the order in which things happened because there were times I stopped listening or else moved away. But there are some scattered snapshots.

We all moved to Boca Raton when I was starting high school. In the guesthouse of the house with the white tiles there, there were samples of flavored

MAGICAL HABITS

tequilas in tiny minibar bottles in the closet. From the boxes of Bubble Wrap I took sample sizes to pack in my purse on my way out the door. I liked the coffee flavor the best because it was smoky and sweet. I didn't think of it as rebellion: it was part of a way to pass the time with friends who didn't ask hard questions when I didn't have easy answers.

Another: in a California Pizza Kitchen, after he no longer lived in the house with white tiles, just before the years when I didn't see him except in photographs, I took bites of Chinese chicken salad between phrases, between syllables. He mostly talked, I mostly didn't listen. With other fifteen-year-olds (and let's face it, sometimes I still do this as an adult), being casual is a form of power. Only later do I admit that this form of power has its costs too.

Another: on a morning there are suddenly five of us in the house with white tiles and tequila samples. Someone is making breakfast, and it's not my grandmother. Do I like fried eggs on toast, he asks? Um, sure. The smallest one of us—a new us—is brand-new and my brother. It's his father asking me about the fried eggs. I wheel my brother around the mall in his stroller, and the Boca Raton shopping mall regulars think he's mine. I leave the next year for college, before he starts to walk. I posed with him in my arms wearing a pointy birthday hat for his first birthday; it's one of the only photographs I have to remind me of that summer.

Another: I get the first email in college and stare at it on the screen of the Sony VAIO laptop that gets too hot if I leave it on all day and burns my wrists if I write for too long. I read the email twice, and crawl into bed because now what? I write back in the hopes that the middle of June could stop being confusing, and so that I no longer feel jealous on Father's Day. I worry about jealousy as though it were a disease and could make my liver and spleen swell. I find out what it feels like to write into silence that answers back intimate words, only to answer back silence sometimes too.

My brother, whom I called Baby for most of his life, and my mom came to visit me a few years ago for Mother's Day. At DePaul, he was a marketing major with a sales concentration. It's not the first time he asks, but I hear it this time with more tenderness, I want to know about Salvador. This is a name he's heard obliquely, part of, in his words, a whole life that you, our sister, and mom had without me. You're so nice, he said, I don't understand how you can say things like that about your father. It is sincere and not pathological curiosity about the person he calls Salvador. And from where I sit that bit is nothing short of a miracle.

That's when my mom tells a story, new to me, from 1985. She had been working at the restaurant and he hadn't been paying her, so that when she asked Tía Celia her advice about getting a divorce and Tía Celia asked, reasonably, Do you have any money? If you leave, you'll need money because you have kids—my mom had to say, No. It was the accountant, my mom tells us, that convinced him that he should pay me for working. (Not history, the constitution, or a conscience.) After that, I had to learn how to hide money so that eventually I could leave. Eventually took a little over ten years.

This book was going into production when I opened a manila envelope that I'd carried around unknowingly in a giant canvas duffle bag since college from move to move and coast to coast. It has some of their restaurant archives in it. In the manila envelope was a typed letter on the Illinois attorney general's letterhead, dated November 1992, addressed to one of the workers at the restaurant whom I've known my entire life. "Enclosed please find the approximate amounts due from Salvador for the following former employees," and then a list of names, signed by the assistant attorney general. There were scraps of paper where people had kept track of how much money they'd been underpaid in the month of October and a "summary of unpaid wages" worksheet from the US Department of Labor.

⟶

Courts have cash registers, it occurs to me, when I hear the cash register shut. Her hair—the one I don't know—brushes my coat as they whisk out of the clerk's office.

In the French Middle Ages, courts of love would have heard the case, both cases, this one about teeth and the one about divorce, which was maybe also about teeth.[1] In courts of love, unlike in other courts, women could appear and the rules of love established the grounds of justice, effectively shrinking the distance between a judge and a poet.

MARCH 2001 *Cambridge, Massachusett homelands*
REVISED JULY 2013 *Brooklyn, Munsee-Lenape homelands*

1976

YOU ARE ON YOUR KNEES. Francisco stopped it before you got there, but the steam is snaking through the grates, as though the air is also sighing.

He had been waiting for you to look inside. This container—the one you are kneeling in front of—accepts cuts of meat from the conveyor belt and grinds them up before the new meat is packaged, refrigerated, and shipped out to markets. On each package, the seal says "Hecho en México" above a furious-looking eagle. If it were in English, there might also be an eagle, but there would be less doubt about whether the phrase marked an event. *Made*, unlike *hecho*, can never be both. And in either language, you'll never know exactly who makes anything happen, or if there are even people to ask. What you can know is a kind of origin: geography, a map in relation to other maps, the fixed points you learn to focus on as the landscape whizzes past. With geometry and imagination, if you change course, eventually you find your way back to square one. It's what happens when you live on a round rock encasing lava.

You don't think about that. You think about the bottom of the container where the meat gets churned, where the walls inside the container spin to shrink muscle, nerve endings, sinews, and bits of forgotten bone into meat and more meat. The twentieth century revered this orchestration of opposing forces, legally binding agreements dressed in shrink-wrap. Quickening as a new promise. You don't think about all the poets who have written eulogies for time.

Like the best ones in Guadalajara, you know the factory is, for the most part, clean. But you also know it can't be helped if one piece or several falls off the conveyor belt, and that sometimes there might be dust. Just like sometimes there is no time to clean: the belts move quickly and it's as common to get paid by the hour as by how much work you do. Then sometimes it rains and the factory—like hunger and heartbeats—doesn't stop for the rain. There is a roof over the machines, but at dinner one night earlier that summer, your father told you the roof had a leak. There are no floors yet, so there's always the chance that when the employees are moving around they might kick dust up into the vat where the meat gets churned. It is before and past the time when reporters actively look for dust in factories with cameras.

There are times when certain stories matter, and times when they don't.

And that doesn't save you from this: in the dust you are on your knees.

You are thinking about how little you come to your father's factory, the rows of aluminum machines, the spray that smells like meat moist from steam and fresh with blood. One time, you came to pick him up; the sky-blue Chevrolet had broken down. Another time, you came to get something for your mother; he handed you a bag and walked away. A third time, you were running an errand and passed by but did not stop in. In the most casual sense, there was nothing in particular to say.

Still, Francisco knows you. He sees you pull up in the mustard-yellow Mustang and knows to open the door, to get out of the way. He's been crying and seems confused. You can't hear him, but he might be speaking. When he realizes you aren't listening, he gets louder, more emphatic, wilder. You barely make out his mouth or that it is moving. He is pointing at the machine, at a ladder propped against the side, at a long, wooden paddle on the ground. He is pointing at the back room, he is pushing his baseball cap up, then down, then back again over his eyebrows.

At some point you stopped being able to see sharply; it happened while driving there that things started to blur. You took Manuel Otero, but should have taken the shortcut, to avoid the traffic trying to get on the Periférico along with an entire city trying to get home for lunch while trying to make a workday incidental to trying to make a life. You make out shapes somewhat, only that there are distinctions between them, and buildings, and height, but not dimension. You know colors by relative brightness. Red is brighter than blue, because you know the colors of the awnings on the side of the road by heart. These are the roads of all your childhoods, even though you spent most of it in Elmwood, outside Chicago. Green is brighter than blue but darker than red. There comes a moment you stop seeing color too.

While driving, it started raining the way it does in Guadalajara in the afternoon during the rainy season. Guadalajara is a desert, after all, and like all deserts, it doesn't know how to swallow the clouds. Instead, the city turns gray for half an hour.

You don't think about whether it is the dust. You don't think about how dust mixes with rain. You don't think about whether there is a desert that surrounds the city, whether if the winds blew hard enough the city might get buried for a thousand years and the spire from the cathedral would poke out of a shallow dune for archaeologists to uncover and then use buildings, streets, and this factory to reconstruct how it is you felt on the day you were on your knees studying ground meat. You don't think about green mountains in other places, or sometimes white, that rain makes the air smell green there, or white elsewhere, that gray might have its own smell. That when you were younger, it smelled like Lake Michigan and car exhaust, like the galantina, like glass that shimmered in the morning while your mother ironed the tablecloth before breakfast, and lights that made shapes at night suspended against the sky.

You get up and pass by Francisco. You never say if you were running or walking because you never say you were there.

Then again you are kneeling, but you might have slipped. Or maybe your knees buckled. You can't remember the last time you kneeled in church. At your first communion you sat against the pew, half-kneeling, half-sitting. Your mother was furious and, near the churro man after the service, while the other mothers were taking pictures of white dresses and lit candles, she struck you across your right cheek. In front of the church with no doors, only arched stone entranceways, something strong in you decided then about kneeling.

You don't know when Francisco opened the side panel of the machine. Either everything is quiet or you still can't hear, but the container is wide open. The habaneros you ate with lunch are still fiery on your swollen tongue. Even after your liver stops being able to produce bile, after your stomach lining has gotten holes in it, after your small intestine swells to block you from being able to eat without pain, you will never be able to stop eating them. You will tell a story about eating habanero sandwiches for lunch to all your friends, and some people who aren't your friends, and also to some people you don't know. You will tell it so often you will forget if it happened, or if you started telling it in the first place, and if you started telling it, you will forget for whose sake it got told. You will love habaneros forever when they swell your tongue so that you start to live in it like real estate so that you remember how to feel strong because you will need endurance to stand it.

But right now, with your swollen tongue frozen, you are kneeling in dust looking at ground meat, and this is when you start to be able to see again.

You can guess how much time has passed since the blades spun because some parts are still whole. One arm is intact. You can make out it is an arm because it is short, and because the hand at the end has three fingers. You stretch toward it, pull it out and place it next to you, palm down, on the ground. You make out bits of fabric mixed in with the meat. The legs are there, in several pieces, some wrapped in fabric. One, then another, you gather them. You are moving slowly, or your body tells you so. You think only, Arm, Leg, Leg, Leg, as though you can keep track of the pieces. As though it makes sense to be counting numbers that won't add up.

You're unsure how to treat them, so you choose to act like each is a new baby.

It is difficult to measure space because you are having a hard time believing in dimension, and that you are awake. Red is brighter than blue. Green is brighter than blue. Red is brighter than green. Brown is darkest.

In preschool, along with learning colors and numbers you also learned how to spell it: S — A — L — V — A — D — O — R. It sounded larger than other names, all the open vowels left room to travel.

You shove meat to the sides of the container, cupping your palms like swimming. Your fingers feel awkward clutching the pieces you recognize, the way it could have been affection. Something unnameable slips from your hands. You reach back in for it and realize there is so much that could just be meat. A few times you cut your fingertips. Red is brighter than blue.

Are you moving fast or slow? And what would it mean to finish? Knee, knee. You sit back on your heels, and wipe your upper lip dry with the backs of your reddened hands—one, then the other. Hand, hand. You repeat all the names you can think of until it sounds like a prayer. The pieces left now are small, and are too confused to call them by a name. Your mother will ask you what you found, and you won't want to tell her that there was no shape of a person to find.

Francisco assumes you've stopped to breathe, but your throat behind your swollen tongue is too tense to swallow, like the space behind your eyes is too tight to see. Brown is darkest. Your shoulders creep in toward your throat—Throat—your chin sinks into your chest—Chest—sinking into your stomach. Stomach. You would like very much to feel your feet. Foot. Foot.

You remain on your knees. You clench and unclench your fists, to heave forward, to reach back, when the first sound escapes. Ay.

9. auctions

Vino hasta su memoria la muerte de su padre, también en un amanecer como éste; aunque en aquel entonces la puerta estaba abierta y traslucía el color gris de un cielo hecho de ceniza, triste, como fue entonces. Y a una mujer conteniendo el llanto, recostada contra la puerta. Una madre de la que él ya se había olvidado y olvidado muchas veces diciéndole: '¡Han matado a tu padre!' Con aquella voz quebrada, deshecha, sólo unida por el hilo del sollozo.

Nunca quiso revivir ese recuerdo porque le traía otros, como si rompiera un costal repleto y luego quisiera contener el grano. La muerte de su padre que arrastró otras muertes y en cada una de ellas estaba siempre la imagen de la cara despedazada; roto un ojo, mirando vengativo el otro. Y otro y otro más, hasta que la había borrado del recuerdo cuando ya no hubo nadie que se la recordara.
—JUAN RULFO, *Pedro Páramo*

IT HAD BEEN CLEANED out for the last time and looked like a museum's storage warehouse instead of a restaurant, with objects piled next to one another, waiting for the next place to be placed. The restaurant's sign outside had first been installed only after extended conversations with the City of Chicago, so that it could hang off the building and perpendicular to it in such a way that it could be legible whether you headed toward or away from Michigan Avenue. That day, whether I headed east toward the lake or deeper into the Loop, the sign for Barro Restaurante Mexicano was upside down, a way landlords signal a tenant's business no longer exists.

We chose the name Barro together (my mom, my sister, me) because it wasn't Salvador—after the divorce we couldn't legally use his name anymore. But also because (1) it was going to be easy for some tongues to say; (2) it would be a teachable moment about Mexican clay; and (3) it was a false cognate for another appropriate word, *bar*.

Along the bar top, wrought-iron iguanas with flecked tongues frozen and outstretched sit in a pile next to two industrial-strength blenders, a stack of takeout containers, and several large, woven baskets, which had been full of individually wrapped peppermints. Plain white plates for appetizer platters, side salads, entrees. Silverware. Someone took the icemaker out from behind the bar and it's sitting there, too, waiting for someone to bid on it. A secret meat slicer from the kitchen is out there, half abandoned, half expectant, like anything that ever finds itself waiting on a shelf. The carved wooden doors they bought in Tlaquepaque have been taken off their hinges. A cherub faces out from each one, surrounded by twirling vines and tilting flowers. They are no longer looking at the corner where Lake meets Michigan, but instead watch over what are now relics.

On a few of the barstools, Aztec-looking ceramic figures huddle together. One ceramic vase in particular is no longer holding fake greenery; it is empty and sitting next to the bar. The dust is new, but the colors are faded as though it has recently been exhumed. Out of its three legs emerge the faces of a carved snake, and above each snake a broad-faced man clutches his knees. Each ceramic man wears a cuff on both biceps and a thick, beaded necklace with a large medallion at the center. The double lines of their mouths are rounded at the edges and pulled perfectly straight, either serious or expressionless, either solemn, or waiting for something to react to, or not animate at all, delineating the visage of a god whose face might never move. What I especially love that day is that I can make out the toes from the four tiny, thoughtful slits carved into their triangulated feet.

What time are people supposed to come?, I ask my uncle, who helped my mom organize the auction. He's having his own relationship with what's accumulated and out of place. After all, it—this—was his life too. In about half an hour. So how does it work? If they want something, they say how much they want to pay. But I don't know how many people will come. Is it mostly people who have their own restaurants? Sometimes. But sometimes just it's

MAGICAL HABITS

people like who bought a house. Oh, okay. I guess that makes sense. Although why would you want an industrial-strength blender in your house?

My mom threw a party the night before, to say goodbye. This was the last restaurant she had held on to. There was another one near where she lived, but a former employee bought it and so freed her from managing it. The way she convinced me to come out from California was to say that the party was a thank-you to Chicago. My sister and oldest nephew were there. I danced, holding him on my hip, while the mariachi and then the DJ played. I had my T-Boz haircut dyed purple then. I chose it to say hello to California. My mom, who in her own nomadic intellectual journeys as an adult had been trained at Pivot Point School of Cosmetology in Bloomington, refreshed the purple dye the night before the party. So that the party was not the first time she'd tried to leave the restaurants, but it was the last time.

In one section of the restaurant, the chairs were arranged in a circle, and the mariachi stood together at the center. Where there used to be a giant poster of a woman in a headdress at the foot of a mountain, that night there was a banner. The poster was from an exhibit in Mexico City that my parents had never been to, but my mom had had it framed for the enormous wall they didn't know what to do with. It was a reproduction of Jesús Helguera's *Popocatépetl y Iztaccíhuatl*. During the Mexican Revolution, Helguera's father, who was a Spanish economist, had fled with his family to Spain. Spain, then, is where Helguera studied painting and married a woman named Julia, whom he would paint many times. Reversing his childhood migration to escape the Spanish Civil War, Helguera took his wife-muse to Veracruz.

One time, because the image was a little racy, I asked what it was. She said, Cerca del D.F., there are two volcanoes. One of the volcanoes is supposed to look like a woman lying down.

Iztaccíhuatl was a princess in love with a warrior, Popocatépetl. After promising that they could be married if Popocatépetl made it back, her father, the cacique of Tlaxcala, sent him off to battle against the Aztecs. Popocatépetl did return, but Iztaccíhuatl was dead. The Mexican government stands by the version where he carries her body up the mountains, lays her across them, and there dies beside her as the snow covers them both. A romance about Tlaxcaltecos that legitimates Aztec rule, it's also a ready-made vehicle for nationalism's selective memory.

The banner that replaced the doomed lovers said, "Thank You for Thirty Years of Business, Chicago!" I sat next to my sister, sometimes looking at her face to see if there was anything to recognize, sometimes thinking about how thirty years was how old I was just then.

In 1961, demonstrating renewed awareness of Chicago's cultural groups (the groups themselves were hardly new to Chicago), the *Chicago Tribune* ran a series of articles featuring Chinese, Mexican, and Puerto Rican residents and "the vast majority of the immigrants who have come to Chicago . . . of European origin." These "new" immigrant groups had "established their own little cultural islands" in Chicago.[1] The reporter notes that "not all of them [Mexicans] can be called immigrants, since some were born in the southwest and are native born citizens. The rest were born in Mexico and came here seeking the fabulous wages they hear about in their native villages."[2] Citizenship here is a technicality rather than a cultural distinction. That is, Mexicanness doesn't go away, regardless of what kind of passport a person might carry.

One of the primary ways the same reporter describes Mexican culture is through their "highly spiced" foods.[3] He takes on a pedagogical stance and goes into great detail discussing Mexican food: "Their menus are built around three staples—tortillas, beans, and beef. The tortilla, which is made of meal of ground corn and baked on a grill, is used much like we use bread."[4] But translating the tortilla into bread is not a simple act of substitution.[5] Instead, doing so shows us that there are many processes at work in making certain food appear as itself, that there is an aspect of performance every time cultural recognition and authorization is "happening." The reporter acts as a cultural guide for readers, presumed to be non-Mexican. By offering analogues for Mexican food—for example, by translating tortilla as a kind of bread—he bolsters his own cultural authority while distinguishing Mexican residents as culturally separate from Chicago, their own "island."

The next year, another reporter visited a "bruising rodeo" to perform the role of tour guide to readers through the "Mexican colony."[6] His opening vignette relates a brief and imperfect history of charros in Mexico:

Charros—or horsemen—of Mexico have been popular heroes since the Spanish conquest in the early 1500s. Throughout Mexico today the charro occupies an unequaled position among his countrymen. And in the big cities of the United States which have Mexican communities, small bands of charros have been organized. These horsemen hold fast to the traditions of their ancestors. . . . Fred Leavitt was among the spectators at a rodeo held recently by the charros of East Chicago [unreadable], at nearby St. John. . . . This is his account of the festivities.[7]

This ahistorical history of charros positioned the "charros of East Chicago" as simply reenacting "the traditions of their ancestors" rather than reinventing them for their new environment.[8] The introduction also situates Leavitt as one of many spectators among the crowd. He writes, "As I stood there watching the pattern of wide-brimmed hats continually change, I felt Mexico." Leavitt "feels" Mexico through the gear these cowboys wear, the "aroma of spicy Mexican food [that] was mixed with the strong scent of leather. A mariachi band played brassy Mexican music, which was accompanied by excited Spanish voices, and the staccato of horses' hooves in the distance."[9]

After Chicano mobilizations in Chicago, in 1977 George Estep writes a *Chicago Tribune* article about La Villa Chiquita.[10] By this time, Chicanos had demanded to be recognized as something other than perpetually foreign.[11] But the word *Chicano* was far from stable; within the Chicano movement there were disagreements about what it meant. Most broadly, it meant Mexican heritage. The article itself is an attempt to account for the economic well-being of La Villa Chiquita. Nonetheless, Little Village is, for him, a tourist location with "visitors who enjoy the restaurants, bakeries, shops, and markets that line 26th Street west of Kedzie Avenue."[12] It is "a bright spot of ethnic color in an otherwise gray area."[13] For Estep, the high rate of homeownership and "a dozen financial institutions and . . . real estate agencies" meant that the community was "a phenomenon of stability and relative prosperity in an area not known for either quality."[14] Estep reproduces the logic that recognition and accomplishment can only be framed as an exception.

The map that accompanies the article defines the boundaries for La Villa Chiquita, including "Western and Cicero avenues, the Burlington Northern railroad tracks, and the Sanitary District Canal."[15] The map's stable boundaries and the confident arrow that locates Little Village within its boundaries exemplifies the perception that the Mexican parts of Chicago are separate from the rest of the city, not unlike the representation of the "Mexican colony" in the earlier article.

The first potential bidder arrives and starts walking around. He is wearing the kind of coat most men in Chicago wear in the winter, a car coat cut short with an elastic band so that it hits just above his hips. It's a strange silhouette for masculinity but keeps warmth centered at the midsection. He eyes the deep fryer for a while. My uncle walks up to him to answer questions. I can't get over the whole scene, a strange garage sale where a meat slicer can hold sentiment. I head back to the bathroom, past two sets of imposing, black columns.

When the space was in the midst of transformation into a Mexican restaurant, the columns still hadn't been painted over. They were green and red with gold capitals. Amid drywall and heaps of wood panels with no particular designation, my dad looked over the columns. We can't take them down. We thought about it, but the engineer said that they hold up the roof. ¡Ja ja ja! So we can't do that. So what I think we're gonna do is set the bar right in the center. They think I am nuts. Why are they painted that color? This used to be a Chinese restaurant. Oh, that makes sense, I guess? It's good because we didn't have to change that much in the kitchen; they had all the equipment. We bought a couple more deep fryers, but they had the walk-in coolers, both of them, and one deep fryer, I guess for like egg rolls. But I was thinking that if we put the bar here we can use the columns. Otherwise, I think they will stand out. I was thinking of covering them up at first, but maybe we just paint them black. Where will you hang glasses from? I don't know yet how we're going to do the overhead for the bar. Maybe just hanging, with like plexiglass from wires. What do you think? That sounds good—but the glasses won't be too heavy? Depends on what wire we use.

In the bathroom, I spend an awkward amount of time staring at the Mexican tiles, patterned with red, blue, and yellow flowers. Once my mom had settled on these tiles, they were the only ones they used in all the restaurants' bathrooms. And there I was, no longer washing my hands, staring at the tile, trying to re-create the childhood trick where I stared at something long enough so that I never forgot it. (That doesn't work.) All that restaurant gear outside, and what I want to keep are these.

When I get back, only a few more people have shown up, one couple that is opening a pizza place in the suburbs near where they live, and another man in a coat with an elastic band at the waist. It seems like there's a lot of interest in the deep fryer, in the blenders, and in the plates. Once it starts, it's not really a bidding war. The blenders get taken for twenty dollars, the deep fryer for fifty. The plates and silverware all for forty.

What happens with everything else?, I ask my mom when she makes her way to the bar. She's been hiding in the kitchen most of the time, pretending it needs to be cleaner. There's a truck that's coming for it. Right, you said that before, but where is it going? I don't know, I told them to take it away. To where? To whoever needs it. You're giving it all away? She laughed. Yes,

I am giving it away, mamita. I don't need it. What would I do with all these chairs? Does it feel weird to you? What do you mean does it feel weird? To see everything like this. To tell you the truth mamita, I am very happy that someone else will have these chairs. They are good, strong chairs. Right, no, I get that—but it's so empty. Of course it's empty, it's not open anymore! Ma, you know what I mean! ¡Ja ja!, I do, I don't know if I feel weird like you said, but I know what you mean. How are you getting sentimental now? You never liked the restaurants.

El Popo y el Izta (affectionately), the two snow-covered volcanoes, are a site for praying to Tlaloc to bring rains. In the early days of 2020, El Popo erupted. It's estimated ash was sent 20,000 feet into the sky.

DECEMBER 2011 *Oakland, Ohlone homelands*
REVISED NOVEMBER 2020 *Philadelphia, Lenni-Lenape homelands*

10. uncertainty and bathing

Not only does she sustain contradictions, she turns the ambivalence into something else. —GLORIA ANZALDÚA, *Borderlands/La Frontera: The New Mestiza*

BEFORE NOW, it was easy to believe in planes of smooth skin with no dimples, no looseness, no folds, no dark hair, no stretch marks weaving patterns across hips, no small, scattered pimples, no scars, no rough patches, no asymmetry, no roundness, no resting places where skin comforts skin. Just clean, empty planes of skin. The kind I imagined in any dressing room, in swimming pools, in the shower in every city on my map. What dreams and fictions have in common is that they can travel with us, follow us around, stick to our bellies, become the way we live.

There was a long, teenage time I wouldn't have dared to look up in the tiled room full of women's bodies lounging beside pools, in saunas and steam rooms, at Kabuki Springs in San Francisco. I would have been too busy wrestling breath from the embarrassment, too focused on the certainty of being seen. But now it's so obviously the case, and another kind of embarrassment to remember I wouldn't have believed it even seeing the bodies: that no two are alike except in the broadest of senses, the ones anatomy turns into drawings that wear hardly any flesh—though not none.

Surrounded now by the sounds of splashing showers and bodies swooshing into pools, my belly dips into my lap. I stretch my legs over a white towel. I am bare and gleaming, and I breathe carefully with my eyes closed. Slow and quiet, I am as sincere as I get, sweating onto the sauna's wooden planks, growing beads of sweat in the familiar places: shoulders, rounded slightly forward, in streams down my back, between my breasts, nipples relaxed, pointing at my top, friendly stomach.

If we loosen the legal fiction that sin, sociology, and statistics helped make, that nakedness means *visible, utter, revealed, stark, known,* and *lusty*—what then? Would questions and mysteries stubbornly reappear and would bodies again feel holy in the sense that they could not be profane.

With Adam and Eve, the story snowballs into the origin of shame and pretends to be the birth of a pernicious kind of humility. The knowledge of good and evil shades pleasure with suspicion. The admonition: always ask what is this and why does it feel good? Build a wall between darkness and light, forget it was all of us who built it and mourn our exile. Keep seeking grace, keep on your knees, even if you never get there, even if you know there is nowhere to get to. A kind of premise was born, where it's better to know and suffer the consequences than to be innocent of choice. The counterlesson is the ability to say *Innocence is bliss* and chuckle. But usually neither redeems anyone. The story that is supposed to work like magic only leaves you in the trenches again, with either a terrible choice or a tragedy.

Maybe they were just disoriented. "And the eyes of them both were opened, and they knew that they were naked; and they sewed fig leaves together, and made themselves aprons." That's the English translation, and the lesson is shame as the proof of distance from the divine. But sight changing could be the ability to say *me* and *mine,* the ability to gauge distance (internal and external), which is not the same as being far—or getting farther—from any god. The "eyes of them both were opened" could mean newness, or could be new focus, not new knowledge exactly: the beginning of understanding the possibility of mistranslation, which is not the same as heresy or lies. Maybe new sight meant *place, here, this, body,* each finally in more than three dimensions. Maybe fig leaves are about safety without presuming danger first, but about acknowledging what's sacred, because if I can distinguish place I can begin to understand elements and start trying to predict the weather. The weather will not always harm me, but I know I should take care. And all of that, of course, is only the beginning, and the only beginning to love, because it is also the beginning of labor, which is never just a beginning in pain, even when it is sure to come. Is there a faith that does not begin from any version of fear? A grito in the wilderness when it's all wilderness.

In the menus and personal stories of restaurant owners, Mexicanness is made to "happen" over and again in an unsettled way, revealing it to be an idea that keeps being reimagined. Their claims to stability in light of the opposite might be understood as "the incurable otherness from which oneness must always suffer." This is the way that Antonio Machado, writing in an early twentieth-century Spain that had yet to be ruled by Franco, wrote against the idea that identities—like food—could or should be singular. For Machado, it is "the incurable belief in human reason" that attempts to fix any identity, where "identity = reality" and "everything must necessarily and absolutely be one and the same."[1] The history of Mexican restaurants in Chicago leads us back to a series of processes that exceed even the ways the categories of sameness and difference construct one another over time. Machado's point, that is, the responsibility of reading with Machado, is not an easy one: to accept that we are all already contaminated with one another.

The experiences of migration, displacement, and seeming to exist "in-between" cultural worlds are paradoxically what give restaurant owners the idea of authenticity to define themselves and their food. Yet, in Chicago's Mexican restaurants, there are no easy boundaries, in the same way that a city exceeds its maps. On Nuevo León's menu cover, what has just arrived? The skyscrapers or the cacti? In the Salvador's logo of a married couple dressed as American pioneers superimposed on the Alamo and, later, an adobe home: who is playing pretend at what and at whose expense? Bahena learned his version of Mexican authenticity from Bayless. Or can Mexicans not learn, and so never change?

William Grimes writes in a *New York Times* article, "Every Mexican restaurant above the taco-stand level must answer a fundamental question at the outset. Will it take the pledge and swear to serve fine food, with a respect for regional differences and prime ingredients, or will it saunter down the cash-strewn path to Margaritaville?"[2] For Grimes, there is a hierarchy of Mexican restaurants, in which taco stands and "Margaritavilles" have less cultural integrity than restaurants "with a respect for cultural differences." The implication is that authentic Mexican restaurants are more respectable than those who "saunter down the cash-strewn path." The desire to make money, for Grimes, jeopardizes a restaurant's cultural authority. Instead of understanding that, in a sense, we all created Margaritaville, it becomes a sign of undesirable contamination. As though in any business, there is a way of remaining pure.

Authenticity is a real value for Grimes, and it's especially present for him when "traditional lava-stone molcajetes" are used to make guacamole.[3] And authenticity is whatever he might decide. What Grimes and others may not realize is that the act of making the molcajete distinctly other is how he stabilizes his sense of self too. Imagine needing to be able to name a molcajete in order to know who you are by way of contrast. It is an exhausting game. For Grimes and for food critics in Chicago, authenticity is a way to reinforce that there are foreign cultures, that there is a value—that is, money to be made by others—in keeping them foreign.

Even beyond that, what Grimes calls "Margaritavilles" once counted as authentic too. Huerta's customers knew that his burritos were authentically Mexican. Authenticity itself—its performance, description, emotional assurances—is the evidence of history and power. But being able to describe authenticity as a kind of dance does not explain or account for the imbalanced power relationships evident in how it is used, or who can decide which is which. All the while, in Mexican restaurants where critics and owners perform expertise and belonging for one another, something like "the other"—who really is of our own making, no matter who we are—lives and thrives amid margaritas, migration stories, and burrito dreams.

I watch footsteps drying on the ceramic tile floor. The fresh swishes from the showerheads behind me dribble to a halt when a hand shuts off the water. The hollow gulps of the warm pool welcoming another woman who needs rest and to feel new and to feel different and to feel like water accepts all the parts she'll fight against tomorrow. I wrap arms around my knees, sitting still on the damp towel draped over a slatted wood lawn chair. I feel them against me, the spaces that make the chair too. Rectangular sections of me droop into them. I breathe with another thought: it's the dim lighting as much as the noiselessness, each body in its own space, emptying out, emptying in, out of habits too numerous and too ordinary to name.

When Charles Darwin wanted to understand facial expressions, he looked at photographs by a French neuroscientist and muscular dystrophy expert named Duchenne and then asked the controversial Swedish photographer Oscar Rejlander to find the instant of an expression before a camera "truly" could.[4] Darwin wanted to figure out what expressions were and where in deep time they came from and why it looks like animals make them, why humans have habits for expressing emotion, and how old or new a spirit would have to be to break them.

It's easy to forget (though Liz Grosz, among others, has reminded us): evolution didn't have all the answers. Natural selection, if it proves something, only proves it after it happened; it is not possible to predict "fitness." What "fitness" means is that a form of life survived over stretches of time. "Fitness," for Darwin and all the evolutionary biologists after him, only happens, can only be attributed afterward.[5] The desire to believe in the human power to direct and decide and engineer is so strong that this aspect of Darwin's findings got rescripted to fit in with much older civilizationalist, capitalist, and racist notions of "development."

There are so many moments in history that prove knowledge is not the same thing as meaning, and that knowledge, even the most honest, can take on an unintended tone. Who would accept approximations and provisional explanations and to forgo the sharp but cozy quiet of certainty? Who can carve meaning—personal or social—from an aggregation of *almosts* and *maybes* and *to the best of our knowledges*? It's a strenuous ask, especially when the weather is changing. It's a lot to risk without very much to hold on to. Except everything. And everything else.

***

I stand up when it's time to stop thinking about other women's bodies, about Darwin and maybes, when it's time to rub mine with salt and turn my skin pink with effort. I think *lymphatic system* with a self-satisfied smile, when I pump it toward my heart, insistent, patient, the salt stinging the places my razor showed its age. By then I'm thinking about how long it can take to bathe if I give myself time: an entire day, the length of a modernist novel, of a conversation about breaking up, of a turning earth turning, predetermined by the wonder that I can need and keep needing to bathe well beyond the moment of getting clean, when I must have remembered someone else's memory that it could be a ritual, when the nearness of water was a basic luxury. Just twenty-five dollars for a full day.

Here everyone else is doing it right. They don't have questions. Or they don't seem to. They only have every form of water at their disposal, even tea. Water to let questions rest for a little while. Water to erase some questions entirely, especially, if it's possible, the stubborn ones. Water to forgive the people who can't forgive their bodies, their round bellies, their wide shoulders, hanging limbs like linens waiting to dry, their tired hips, and lower stomachs that keep their upper stomachs company.

In a world of radical difference, certainty is a posture about knowledge rather than the tender knowledge itself. Certainty asserts sameness. As such, certainty does the work of affects more than living in the relations knowledge can bring us into.

More strenuous than an argument, which shuts down the world into itself no matter how expansive its gaze, is writing knowing someone else, all else, has to keep going.

JULY 2012 *Brooklyn, Munsee-Lenape homelands*
REVISED NOVEMBER 2020 *Philadelphia, Lenni-Lenape homelands*

2010

"I HAVE TO SHOW you the videos; they're on my Blackberry—I just have to remember who sent them to me. Hold on a minute.

"Okay, there they are: look at them in order. They should be numbered, are they numbered?

"So what happens is that the machine actually takes the cactus fruit whole. No, without washing them or anything. You just feed them into the first machine, and the machine washes the cactus fruit. You should see it! The mothers and the kiddies from the town, they all come to the factory to drop off cactus fruit. The grandparents.

"No, there's a shitload of them! There's so many tunas lying around people don't know what to do with them. Most of the time they would just rot there. The problem used to be that there wasn't an easy way of peeling them, and taking the seeds out, so they would just rot on the floor, piles and piles of them. And—you've eaten a tuna right?—the seeds aren't like in a papaya or something, in the middle that can easily be scooped out, with a tuna they are throughout the entire fruit, like a watermelon or a blackberry. And with cactus fruit, which is also different from other fruits, you don't want to throw away the seeds. No, because the oil from the seeds is really expensive. Beauty companies, like L'Oréal and Revlon, big companies like that, they use the oil from the cactus fruit seeds in their products and pay lots of money for it. I don't remember exactly how much but it's something crazy, like a hundred dollars for a quarter-ounce.

"I'm serious!

"Yeah, look at the videos and see how we do it. They get washed, then the little tunas pass a little further down and get peeled, one by one. The peel goes one way, and the inside of the tuna goes down the other shoot. The peel, we grind it up and make animal feed. Really. We had to show the government that we were thinking about the environment—that's good for them—and so being able to say that we used every single part of the tuna was really important. That was the only way to get the tax breaks.

"Then the inside part, which is pulp, and juice, and seeds, here's the part that makes this different from all the other ways of working with the tuna. The machine takes the seeds right out and can separate them. Then we can press the seeds for the oil. From that point on, it's like any other machine that works with a lot of fruit. It takes the fruit, now that all the seeds are out, and it crushes them and separates the juice from the pulp. From the juice we make the brandy and the wine, then the seeds can get sold, then from the pulp we can make jellies and jams. It's really cool!

"Oh, it's delicious. No, no, you gotta try it. The brandy we keep in these huge oak barrels. And for the wine we use birch, because of the different flavors that it gives each. And because of the amount of time that it's gotta stay in there before it's ready.

"We went to our first exposition a few months ago, and people really loved it. Oh, that's right, I sent you the picture of one of the stands. Everyone loved it! They went nuts. 'Absolutely unbelievable,' they were saying. Unbelievable. Because no one's ever done it before. No. They are a nothing fruit. No one has been able to make all the different products you could make out of them because they couldn't take the seeds out conveniently. It was too labor intensive, you know. But now, aw, man! It's just incredible.

"Well, that's how we got the Mexican government involved. First, we had to show them that the technology worked, that it was not messing with the environment, and that we were planning on being able to give jobs to all those people.

"Of course it's a job! It pays like a job, but even way better than any job. And they didn't even have a bad job before: grandmas and kiddies. And we pay each of them the exact same. We pay them by the pound. The grandmothers come with baskets and baskets of them. The kids use their little wagons, and sometimes just in their arms, as many as they can carry. They come up to me, crying, thanking me. It feels weird. The only other time I felt like that was when we were doing the Ozono project. Do you remember that one?

"Las gotitas, yeah. To try it out, 'cause you know I didn't believe them. I thought, 'Yeah, right! These little drops can cure cancer!' So, to test it out, through Marcelo—you remember the one who runs the hospital in Guadalajara?—we gave the gotitas to the Centro Médico in Guadalajara, to give to the little kids who had cancer. We knew for sure it wasn't going to hurt them at all, so why not? And then they told me how much better they were doing, and I still didn't believe them. I wanted to see for myself. So Prudenica and I visited one of the floors with the kids one time, and they were all crying, and thanking us. One of the mothers said that I saved her child's life. It was wild.

"Yeah. So we pay them per pound, and then we make them partners in the company, so that they will have a share in the profits. It's not a huge amount, but it's way more than they make otherwise, especially like the grandmothers. So we're helping the government look good on both ends, and they give us a tax break for having the factory in Morelos instead of somewhere else.

"But it's my biggest project because of the financing. I am also the financing!

"I mean that I am going to buy a bank. Soon, it's the last part of how we are going to make this work. I'm going to buy a bank in Guadalajara. I have partners, but you know how people are. They don't want to take risks. And you need to be able to take risks. So I'm putting up all the capital. Something like twenty-five million dollars. It will be ready by then. We took a hit a couple years ago, but in not too much longer I should be ready to go. Once we have the bank, the rest is going to be a piece of cake. We already did all the work, we already built it, we already know it's great, we already know we are helping people, we just have to start the engine!

"I feel like this is the one. It's a combination of everything—the restaurants, the margarita, the leasing companies, the Ozono—and it's helping people. You really should see their faces. The next time you come to Guadalajara, I'll take you so you can see their faces. Man, this is the one. It's the project I'm most proud of, the one I'm going to leave behind. The other stuff, the restaurants, the margarita, the leasing companies, even the tequila. It was kids' stuff compared to this.

"This is the one. Like my masterpiece. ¡Ja!

"Yeah, I get to rest sometimes. The doctor doesn't think I should be running around so much; you know, my legs get swollen like you wouldn't believe sometimes, but it's what I do.

Interview with local Spanish television station

c. 1987
Author's personal collection

Blank Beta tape

2013

"PRUDENICA KNOWS EVERYTHING that happened. But most of it, I didn't have to tell her because she was there. She was there and she saw it, she saw me and how fucked up I was. I had lost everything. Everything, everything. I didn't have nothin'—again, like when I started when I was young.

"I don't know what made me go back to the margarita then or back to the restaurants now, so long later. It was something I knew I could do, and do well. Sometimes you can't experiment, and you should never wait around to see if something falls in your lap. That's never going to happen, nothing falls in your lap. You have to move. You have to choose and then move. It's simple. Nothing makes me crazier than watching people wait around for someone to give them permission. For what? That and people not knowing what they want. I never understood that. How could you not know? Who else will know?

"It was what I knew, so we got on a plane. We went everywhere; I called everybody. People thought I was crazy—again. ¡Ja! But I didn't care. I tell these young guys, you have to believe that strongly in something, you have to close your eyes, and focus, and know that it's going to happen. Maybe I'm a little weird. To these young guys, I talk to them, and they are so much smarter than I was at their age, and they know so much more, went to so many more schools than I did, but they have these limiting ideas—they can come from anywhere, from their mother, their father, their wife, their high school football coach. People limit themselves all the time—I don't like watching it. I get so frustrated.

"So the ones that come to me, I talk to them. I try to figure out what keeps them blocked, and tell them to stop right away. Don't even decide, just stop. Choose something else, move, commit everything to something. That makes it matter. You can stay wondering forever and ever and still have no fucking idea where one of those beliefs came from. Does it matter? Let it go. Build a new belief. Dream about something else. Decide. It doesn't matter what the decision is.

"Now, I don't even have to tell myself to focus, I just focus, and I can feel myself putting all my energy, all my little brain waves, everything, everything, everything into it. And I did that. I didn't think about all the million and one things and the million and one reasons why it wasn't going to work, wasn't going to happen, all the people who thought I was wasting my time. I just focused; in the middle of my forehead I could feel all that energy. I pictured what I wanted.

"What did I want? ¡Ja ja ja! If I tell you, it loses the magic—like a birthday wish. ¡Ja! But trust me, I knew. Yeah, I got some of it. Like what? Like I made the margarita successful enough to sell it to a new distributor—again. Absolutely! JetBlue still serves Salvador's Margarita. Next time you're on JetBlue, ask for a margarita, and they will give you Salvador's.

"Then ten years ago we moved to Guadalajara, so I could retire. Why? Because I was tired! No, I'm not that old, but my father had this great saying: Lo que cuenta no es el modelo sino las millas recorridas. I feel like that. He also said, Más sabe el diablo por viejo que por diablo. I think that's my favorite one now that I'm an old man.

"Fifty-nine. Today I'm fifty-nine years old. ¡Ja ja ja! Un-fuckin'-believable. I never thought I would make it this far. I'm tellin' you, it's completely true: no es el modelo, sino las millas! Can't you tell? Look at all this! We've traveled a lot of miles!

"Now, New York Burrito Company. It's wild, I never thought I would do restaurants again, but I saw the whole thing before I even decided to do it. I told my daughter on the phone, I think this is the thing, the one Big Thing that I'm going to do in my life. All the other stuff was just play compared to what I think this could be. We're starting them here in Guadalajara. That's right, the King Kong burritos; it's half a kilo of meat. You should see these things! And we sell curly fries, I think we're the only place in Guadalajara you can get curly fries. So we're starting here in Guadalajara, and then next year we'll expand to Puerto Rico and other Latin American countries.

"These burritos, man, you gotta try 'em. It's not just that it's a lot of meat— and half a kilo, do you know how much that is?—it is a *lot* of meat. But we also have specialty meats we make the burritos with. So usually when you have burritos, you think of the leftover meat. That's how tacos and burritos became food for workers. Not a lot of people realize that. A burrito isn't a meal the way chiles rellenos is a dish, or mole is a dish that families have in their homes, or pozole or menudo when you are hung over. Mexicans started eating burritos so they could take the leftovers to work the next day, so they could take an entire meal to work and not have to worry about how to take it. Think about it, it's the perfect working food because it's so portable.

"What we do at New York Burrito Company is stay at the same price point, and give our customers burritos de marlin, de camarón, that's shrimp, de chorizo, that's Mexican sausage, de vegetales, yes! Veggie! That's for the tourists and the moms. It's in style now in Guadalajara to eat healthy, so we made veggie burritos for the moms and the girls who come with their boyfriends after they go out to the bars at night. Yeah, yeah, we're open twenty-four hours. It reminds me of one of my first restaurants. The one that was on Dearborn. Have I told you about that one? With the boa constrictor that would eat the grande burrito? Sometimes when I am there late, I think about that big snake, and I wish we had one. The kids would love it!

"Lots of competition in the city for fast food. But you know what? I love it.

"No, Prudenica won't let me eat there every day. But sometimes I sneak out, and I can get myself some tacos al pastor, with the slices of pineapple that's been roasting all day, and has caramelized edges. ¡Uy uy uy! That's good. But that's not all I eat. Most people that's what they eat every day, or at least every other day and they are happy, perfectly happy to be limited. Or, it's limited to me. I can't eat the same thing every day. Look at me! I haven't eaten the same thing a day in my life, not the same and not a little. Well, besides habaneros. ¡Ja ja ja! I'm the same way with my businesses as I am with my food.

"But I know, it's like I tell my daughters, 'I can't worry about it, I gotta take it easy.' It's just: te tiene que valer madre. That phrase, it's the biggest Mexican secret there is: *Vale Madre*. It means you gotta just relax, enjoy yourself, and not give too much of a shit: te tiene que valer madre. Simple as that. If I look around, no matter what's going on in politics, what's going on in our families, what the narcotraficantes are doing, how many people died that day because they got shot, or were hungry, what we have or don't have, how much the peso has been devalued that year, how corrupt politicians are, how many kids want to sell us chicle at the stoplights because they are the only ones who can work in their family, or their parents left them and they can't remember where they are from—no matter what, we can all just relax and be happy, have a beer—or better, some tequila. ¡Ja!

MAGICAL HABITS

"It's real easy. . . . You gotta just take it all real, real easy. Nos vale Maaadrrrrre. That's real freedom. Americans don't have that kind of freedom.

"¡Ja ja ja! That's right! After all, it's only money, honey!"

[Author's note: There is a New York Burrito Company in Mumbai. It is not likely that Salvador Huerta owns it.]

ii. after hypervigilance

There is a Quichua riddle: *El que me nombra, me rompe.* Whatever names me, breaks me. The solution, of course, is "silence." But the truth is, anyone who knows your name can break you in two.
—CARMEN MARIA MACHADO, *In the Dream House*

BEFORE I ENCOUNTERED the old idea of the invisible city of the wise, before I read Lawrence Selden "challenge" Lily Bart to look for and find the "republic of the spirit" because that was the thing, at least a decade before I read my first tarot card, before I started referring to my astrologer, to my therapist, to my acupuncturist, to my Reiki healer, before I learned that, on the other hand, it could all be attributed to AgRP neurons in my hypothalamus—before all of that, and one by one, I found them. Even though proteins and stories existed when I couldn't name them, I watch out now for becoming a well-intentioned narcissist. What's after hypervigilance?

A friend warned me early: Because if you're just worried about what's wrong with you, you're still only thinking about yourself, and what's the point of that? We met in California when we both needed to spend time on the couch watching *Gilmore Girls*, dipping chunks of Whole Foods's Herb Slab in olive oil sprinkled with Parmesan cheese. California is exactly where to go, I found out, to make daily quests from simple acts of fulfillment and to have everyone nod in approval because they are also on that journey. What I haven't decided is whether it's fair to think all the bits of fulfillment can make you "too soft." It sounds like a puritanical injunction, and those should, according to joy, be met with bristling suspicion.

I asked a friend who is a banker in New York to explain all of finance in the few minutes before our movie started—*naturally* he is a banker, I could say. It is in Harvard's nature to make bankers. I decided that night, when we were seeing *Iron Man 2*, that it was time I understood how the make-believe of money worked as more than a fairy tale. Holding a fistful of popcorn to my mouth, I asked sincerely, So in 2007 and 2008, did the pie get smaller, or did the value go elsewhere? I don't understand. Because here's the thing: if matter is neither created nor destroyed—and I don't know if money works like that, and my guess is that it mostly doesn't but it's a principle I can get my mind around—but if matter is neither created nor destroyed, I don't understand. So many have less now. And if that's the case, where did some of all of it go? And if it was never there—and I really might be speaking nonsense now . . . seriously, stop me if I am—then how do we know that what we think is there *now* exists? What if the pie right now is like the pie in the past and is smaller than we think? How can anyone make good decisions if all the best information about the money that exists in the world is suspect? These were my questions, and he got very serious. Years later, he's come to a conclusion: markets are not smart. He repeats it like a spell a banker would not cast.

What happens is that objects that stand still are attractive while they tell us stories and while we tell stories about them—like food. Money won't do that, the numbers on tickers remain dancing in the binary code of up or down, and this friend over popcorn told me that the number, when it flashes, isn't even what it says: it stands for a potential future that might only exist as a form in the present as our desire for it in the future. It's a little bonkers. And if that's the case, even if I don't know very much about finance, I do know desire arises only out of an idea of what's missing. Sianne Ngai thought *confidence* was capitalism's tone, but then what's this that sounds more like *yearning*?[1] For me, aspiration, a form of desire, exists between my sternum and throat. No one can see it, and no ticker measures its potential energy. What is less clear is how the accumulated desire (desperation is a tortured flavor of desire) of no one named or seen, when it's gone, makes depressions. Depressions we all feel. I look at him sincerely, That sounds like the business of storytelling.

Value started to exist as the future feeling of no one in particular when ships filled with people for sale sailed west (and east, though fewer remember those) and crossed an ocean, many millions of no ones in particular, and many millions of everyone that could be gotten. The question the future feeling had to answer was, What if the people for sale got sick or died or jumped and couldn't be sold? Morbid, but nonetheless the case: the certainty that some people would die became the engine for a market that spanned oceans but lived in imaginations just as firmly as on lands. Someone needed to get paid for the time it took to round those up who would not get paid, who would stay taken, for the space on the boat that could have been used for barrels of some other instead. Before these ships, a piece of paper could be a promise, but it was just then—with stolen people who became a promise of money even if they died (and so many millions were going to)—that a piece of paper and a signature turned into future money and desire that existed only after an ocean was crossed. That's as much as I know about how money became something I would have a hard time understanding because it wouldn't sit still, because it was fueled (in the sense that it became itself) by the anxious inevitability of death, but more precisely, of murder. Does *profit* sound different if we hear it as proof many suffered? And it makes sense—modern money had to cross an ocean; what's more modern than crossing an ocean with death in your wake, and more murder in your horizon? Modern money made ghosts from feelings and people, from beating hearts repeating their own name.

When he's explaining the last global economic crisis (we were *confident* about the next one, but might not have guessed it would be tied to a pandemic), he doesn't mention the ships, but explains in a way no one on TV could manage at the time of the crash. The way the tragedy went then was that no one, not even the bankers, understood what had happened. He says, Part of it was that there *was* a bigger pie then, but a lot of the value that existed was expected future value; and *that* was what turned out not to be there after all, so the pie shrunk.

Dude, I responded, that's the definition of heartbreak.

Ben Franklin would recognize us as his children: an entire generation that makes lists as though needing to climb out from somewhere or to somewhere but not knowing which is the impulse and not wasting time to figure out if we saved or earned the penny. There are charts, and charts about lists, posts and articles about lists, and lists of articles, and places, and tags, and debris, and sarcasm. One long rope ladder made from teeny tiny bite-size scraps, as if the basic principle of the universe was addition. We've listed ourselves into sounding off the same counted characters of wit and made the caps lock key a substitute for insight, irony, desperation. Ben would even recognize our systems for making sense and for counting down to one: that one time, that one meal, that one kiss. These kinds of equations soften the sting in a moment, but the most quiet is right in the middle, before the equals sign, before a horizon settles, before I become its vanishing point, just before I start looking back to check my work.

All our feelings felt in public on the assumption that that makes them real, and truer, and more noble. Staging our vices with our virtue right out in screens of public and everyday to make what doesn't matter matter because it's safe and unimportant or safe and not surprising or safe and shocking because we've seen it so many times before. It shocks all of us, together, and that becomes enough, even if it can also become a perpetual wound, violences seen every day, multiple times a day, on an endless, maddening loop. The immersion in both cases—stagings of egos and recordings of murder and abuse—can become like knowing. Sontag was right both times: it can make us numb, it can make us move. Then we might unhold it all in close-ups to show we don't need to hold them close, or as a habit of trying to survive. Or take pity on each other and not repost another one but tell you the story and say the name. I want to ask why and what are we doing to each other and ourselves, do we understand how feelings morph to affect the rest of a day when we scroll through every kind of human suffering and hilarity in the ten minutes we're waiting for something, and as we swim in all this too much. Of course, I do it, too, and have neither polite nor impolite answers, just the question and the addiction. And the accumulated fury that we recycle and replenish the perversion of a value (a value!) made possible by so many modern forms of slow murder. And the accumulated fury that there stop being any more names to say to say to say their hearts should still be here and beating.

Sometimes on Sundays, when I lived in New York again, my friend and I read each other's tarot spreads and built something like shelter from numbers and patterns and the fables the ancients wrote with the stars, incorrectly and to great effect. My Google calendar keeps track of the lunar cycle, and I sync it with writing deadlines, to chart when I might feel full and when I might feel new and when I might have no choice but to finish another chapter. There are worse habits than seeking the rhythm of cosmic bodies.

In the red-orange palace in the Spanish mountains that enchanted Washington Irving centuries after it had been neglected and long before tourists stood in line for either the morning or the afternoon entrance: there, Ferdinand and Isabella sat at the center of the Salón de los Embajadores in high-backed chairs while an unproven Genoese weaver-turned-sailor, backed by the centuries-old circuit of Italian capital in Spain, stepped into a moment when the Spanish Crown sought unification and asked rulers that were not his to fund a voyage west. Many others had rejected him.[2] In a corner of the same Salón, I stood quietly at a window set deep into horseshoe arches. The shape of them was then already trying to forget where the arches came from, and why they're still here, under a ceiling of eight-pointed stars carved into wood, placed inside so many tiers made of squares.

What an architecture of geometry within geometry does to seeing when it's what everyone is used to looking through I don't know yet. What relationship to light do people cultivate when it peeks through so many carved corners, making smaller and smaller shapes on the wide floors? Does light become part of the building, part of what hands touch, instead of what to look past, instead of a language for the possibility of looking but at something else? And does that close and open the skies at the same time? Do we need to make light a part of our architecture to feel responsible to the sky? All so unlike the straight lines and sanitary aspirations of the shapes of Chicago's skyline, part of the same fictive West (we find direction by forgetting the round world), where belief in intricacies became belief in mystery, where the substance of light became either geometry or heresy and, no matter what, one has to make a choice. Only one king can have your allegiance, when allegiance is understood as a matter for earthly war instead of enmeshed in unbroken relations.

There is a palace near the Salón where the same Moors that inspired generations of Spanish poets ruled. There are deep blue hints on the walls to squint at, to make visitors look for original tones under centuries of breathing and passing by. That there's so much of any blue left is the promise and the trick of time, the promise of recovery, the trick of lasting enough to make believe. This is the hall of the two daughters; two giant pieces of marble give the room its name. Poetry inscribed in Arabic on the walls is even more proof of all the unseen layers: "Oh, Mohammed, my king, I try to equal / the noblest thing that has ever existed or will ever exist. / Sublime work of art, fate wants me to outshine every other moment in history. . . . The stars wish to rest there . . . "

I walked out into the courtyard that he would have walked out into after Ferdinand and Isabella said yes. He would have walked out with exuberance and relief into imminent destruction. His blunder and its vicious aftermath gave me more than history to call my own, a way to be the ocean and back and a way to dissolve geography, ecosystems, as though all of it was where I'm from not because of any feature on my face or hidden structure that appears as tone, but in the way Wendi Moore-O'Neal, an organizer with and codirector of Southerners on New Ground, put it: "You belong where you are breathing."

And what remains is relations need forms of fiction to become alive, stories to make them true, to fill out an embrace. Give me other stories and I'll hold them together with you. Responsibility comes with kin, no matter how estranged, and the care that might be received grudgingly but still needs to be offered and offered again if we ever get to somewhere else than the somewheres and dead ends that began, for one, in the Sala, it's because enough will insist we don't need anyone—not one not any—to say thank you.

In cities called New York and Chicago, four hundred years after the afternoon that gave me specific, countless ancestors, pageant floats celebrated genocide and electricity, like a king and queen. Westinghouse had won the bid to light the Chicago exhibition, and all Edison had to show for it was a float with tiers of circles of women and twinkling light bulbs. The copper wires that Edison's direct current electricity used were more expensive; Westinghouse undercut his offer by half. As long as you weren't Persian, the rule went, you could wear light bulbs like jewelry and wire like gold. Just like at the bodega, I might have been mistaken for Persian then and not allowed to dress in technology's big jewels. So many hovering lights first cut against what there would be to believe in if something besides the sun kept us awake, and now what we may have forgotten is how to rest, how to pray a prayer for the "stars [that] wish to rest." What's been practiced instead is how to wish upon them, which is to say, ask for things.

My Middle English professor told me in graduate school part two about a medieval manuscript in which a page listed various names for rabbits.[3] This was a not-yet-monolingual print culture. She said scholars in their studied wisdom had yet to figure out what it means that someone copied the list alongside ballads and prayers and naughty vignettes. *Rabbit. Hare. Bunny. Floppy. Cottontail. Long-ears.* Do we keep reinventing the impulse to believe in the magical power of the word: if I know all your names, then you are mine. We make the folklore of Adam and Eve, Borges, Ben, and Freud all proud at the same time for the same reason.

11. AFTER HYPERVIGILANCE

137

There are moments for legends and romance, even others for a morality play, and others for smaller stories, the kind I can hold in my palm, and keep warm, and then put away to find again when I need it, when I'm needed, when it needs me, when you ask. If you ask, I'll say it for you. We can say it at the same time.

➡

I have different ways with each of my friends of talking about and finding the right story for the moment. Sometimes, it's about transformation, about fire, and creation as the need to consume, and find an end. Other times, I want to steer clear of transforming and that nameless space between desire, need, and hope that can pop up every time I look at the ocean and it calls me. If being human means any one thing, it means I need simple things like sleep and love and warmth. Another vanishing point for a transference of pulses and elements. Because if the earth is turning, unsuspended, we already live in space and there is no single, solitary, isolated globe except the ones made into nightlights, the ones teachers hang on bulletin boards, the ones traced onto maps from what cartographers can disremember, like dust and wind and heat. What we sail in are spaceships too, and all the frontiers so named before and after any single voyage give violence some of its reasons.

Other times I am in conversations about silhouettes, dark, bare branches reaching against winter, about a cold wind and a life built up around the fragile words that make themselves available like lifeboats. There are some honest mistakes and there are icy perfectionists, and one trick is where to find compassion when it's hiding and I need it for the accidents that are bound to happen and make me wonder if there really are accidents, because what about all this mysticism? Or there's no need for a modernist nostalgia for a world that existed the way reflections do in movies, a world pretending having ends means that it was ever whole. What if the architecture of belief lives in even the most practical scheme, the most well-laid plans? Should we make some anyway? Can hopeful words repeated often enough make them true? No, Monica. The trick is there is no trick. But, Fred Moten would say, shit do *go* together.[4]

Then there are other times that are not about listing or wondering, at weddings, college reunions, around a piano someone always somehow knows how to play, in the living rooms of East Bay apartments I lived in, in private rooms of karaoke bars in Manhattan, K-town, Oakland, London, Los Angeles, on the veranda of my father's house in Guadalajara before he files for bankruptcy (so he said) and has to try to sell it (so Facebook said). Words marked out in neon time against the backdrop of a music video that doesn't match them, while we act out the life-sustaining fantasy that the song by that one band can cast a spell for three and a half minutes. Was it Chicago? Or Mr. Big? Pat Benatar or George Michael? Whitney? We decide to celebrate all the things we won't solve, even with words even in neon. It's not original, it's not invention, it's not critical, although sometimes we can find the right tone or shape. And there are times when it works how it can work, which is what it means to be working.

There might be reasons questions stay open, and at least one of them is so that we can decide to take them with or walk past them; picking one over another is how to stake a claim to historical time, even when historical time has made a claim on you. It's mine. And another is so that joy might (joy only ever *might*—one of joy's secrets is that it will not obey rules for predicting) explode into the spaces that forgetting—that sneaky bird—can carve out with its tiny, sharp beak. The choice isn't between oblivion and elsewhere after all.

My friend asked—because I was leaving New York again—where home was, and I said, I guess where my clothes are . . . No! Wait, that's too easy. Maybe something like the memory of the house where I learned to play the flute. It was a barely pink brick house with a half-moon driveway and a bean-shaped pool with a diving board and a slide, and I was proud of the fact that we had two chimneys even if we never used either one. It's where I learned to play Hide and Keep like peekaboo with dolphins and photographs and sailboats that disappear in the winter. Where I started listening like breathing.

Where are you from? Chicago. I answer *Chicago* so anyone can hold the story still while we shake hands. It's a habit so many of us have. Oh really, where in Chicago? Southwest suburbs, right off the Stevenson. Near Oak Brook Shopping Mall—but I haven't lived there since I was thirteen. And in another way, Chicago should have never been there. *Where are you from*, as though there is a neat beginning, middle, and end in one city or town, if you've asked yourself to be responsible to more than just what feels good from the oceans and migrations and genocide and rape and dispossession and betrayal and revolution and reinvention and veneration and selling tacos with stereotypes and believing in American Dreams and unlearning nostalgia and keeping heartbreak close and far at the same time and slowing music down and playing Hide and Keep and taking cumulative reviews seriously and studying each fascia gliding just under muscle tissue and lonely nighttimes and cardboard boxes with my name on them ripping again with the force of ripping up the packing tape, cuddling close to the edge of existing as an idea, chasing down an end (history's last loose thread) like it could collapse space-time and coming up empty-handed. Hi, my name is Monica. A placeholder.

But also, What are you? Such a weird, betraying question. That is, they betray—that is, reveal—themselves. I say, Mexican. Oh, really? Yes, really. You can hardly tell!, with relief dressed up as excitement as though any of it is a compliment, as though I was ever in hiding. You mean *you*.

But Chicago is big enough for a single handshake, and if there's a good moment later, I can tell them the fairy tale about the magical burrito who cried for a thousand thousand years when the evil sorcerer Narratio took away his magic and memory and left him lost, wandering in a strange, unmagical land. There are a million ways the end could go, but the way that I tell it, the story ends when the burrito casts off Narratio's spell and becomes magical again. Magical the way burritos float between there and here, between a cheap, exquisite, comforting, and lonely kind of nurturing food. It's not easy to share a burrito without destroying it. It's nearly impossible to eat a burrito without clutching it as though for dear life. Magical because he discloses the need for stories and/as comfort and exists—undeniably—anyway. In another version, the burrito falls in love and marries a wrap without ever figuring out he is a burrito. He has a happy, healthy, blissfully ordinary, wrappy kind of life in Somerville, Massachusetts. I heard someone else tell that he lives in East L.A., working day and night for the revolution to come. He does not sleep much, because the revolution is coming and because he DJs weddings and barbecues on the side. Or, and this is maybe the best version, he takes on a superhero identity to fight failures of imagination, maintaining his cover as a digital sales associate living in a brownstone on the border of Bed Stuy, just where the artisanal cheese and gluten-free-cookie coffeeshops once ended. Archaeologists are going to have a hard time understanding our temples.

When you eat a burrito it can look like you're praying.

A friend said adulthood was about the things you choose not to do. How sad, I answered. I have a restless heart. I heard it as an injunction not against critique but against not considering the position from and toward which a question wanders. There is a habit of not being able to leave well enough

MAGICAL HABITS

alone. A habit that there is so much that deserves careful attention. A habit that attention is the only place pleasure lives. A habit that making power visible could be a pivot to more. Every choice has costs, and so which to take on to chisel the how or why or what or when or who of choice and not choice? Adulthood is a kind of fiction (I have a restless heart), but maybe these small habits are not.

Then again, every single time, why dig through all of history to find the loose seam, to reinvent the world that already existed? Maybe there are times to put away the telescope, and if there's a trick it's to know the difference between when and when and for whom. Even though we know vision is unstable and works like a kaleidoscope in reverse, putting all the fragments together. It's going to mean finding another way to think about invention, like that it's happening all the time but not because we choose it, so can we stop writing stories about how only humans and their cognates are heroes? Or could it be (How can we know for sure? Even our digital maps are just pictures) that stars *do* pause to breathe, to forget and never remember how long they have not been waiting to be found, and maybe the moon *does* slow Time down until they all catch up, maybe the Sea of Tranquility hushes for less than an instant, like a photograph, and you have to take it.

Maybe that's a need to spend a life trying to meet: one extra breath. Maybe that's the beginning of magical thinking: reckoning with an honest sliver, fighting another need we most often think of as suffering, which ends if it ends with letting go (which never ends).[5] Maybe that's what keeps magic—the hope in magic—here and alive and important. If we were already to have breathed it. Then what, what then. Maybe all of it.

If for no other reason than magic spells, like places, like stages, like shapes, like feelings, like heartache, and yesterday: if they're going to be more than wind, pulse, a ghost, they begin for us with a name. *Cottontail*. We should really have more compassion for this bit. It's one piece of how I need you—no matter it too often becomes something else. In the next moment comes the time to let it go. This happens less often.

Even if my name only means mine when someone else says it short, I'll say it for you. If you let me (please let me), I'll let it go for you too.

NOVEMBER 2001 *Oakland, Ohlone homelands*
REVISED MAY 2014 *Brooklyn, Munsee-Lenape homelands*

2017

11:32

Salvador Huerta

SEP 1, 2017 1:56 PM

Hola Moni Quiero ir a visitarte, quieres??

3:34 PM

Si no quieres it's ok

👍

SEP 2, 2017 3:26 PM

Moni, se que estás muy ocupada pero no más tienes que decir No y no te molestó hasta si algún día quieres verme, no hay ningún problema

Aa

12. choreography

Quiero hacer contigo / lo que la primavera hace con los cerezos.
—PABLO NERUDA, "14," in *Veinte poemas de amor y una canción desesperada*

IN AUGUST 1835, the *New York Sun* published a series of phony excerpts by Sir John Herschel, a renowned English astronomer, from the *Edinburgh Journal of Science*. The journal had gone under two years before. Herschel once called Darwin's theory of evolution the "law of higgledy-piggledy" to prove once and for all that scientists could be silly. The *Sun* "reported" that Herschel, while stationed at the Cape of Good Hope, saw creatures living on the moon through his fictitiously enormous telescope. In the stories, Pretend Herschel (really it was Richard Adams Locke) wrote about the life he witnessed on the moon:

> They averaged four feet in height, were covered, except on the face, with short and glossy copper-colored hair, and had wings composed of a thin membrane, without hair, lying snugly upon their backs, from the top of their shoulders to the calves of their legs. The face, which was of a yellowish flesh color, was a slight improvement upon that of the large orang outang [sic], being more open and intelligent in its expression, and having a much greater expansion of forehead. The mouth, however, was very prominent, though somewhat relieved by a thick beard upon the lower jaw, and by lips far more human than those of any species of *simia* [sic] genus.[1]

The story, published over the course of six days, was part of how Locke, a Cambridge graduate and newly arrived to the United States, was going to

Digital reproduction of lithograph of "Vespertilio-homo" on the moon. Originally printed in the *New York Sun*, August 31, 1835; reproduced in Vida, "The 'Great Moon Hoax' of 1835," 434.

help Benjamin Day's penny-press publication become a true competitor to James Gordon Bennett's *New York Herald*.[2] For this accomplishment, of convincing people for at least a week or two that there were indeed many manners of life on the moon, Edgar Allan Poe referred to Locke as a man of "unquestionable genius." P. T. Barnum called the hoax "the most stupendous scientific imposition upon the public," which is to say: game recognize game.[3]

There's so much I love about this story: that it's called the "full moon hoax" or the "great moon hoax," that the newspaper didn't lose any readers when the hoax was discovered, that sometimes when our fantasies get unveiled we stop short of indignation and prefer to host the fantasy anyway. The *Sun* even published drawings of what Pretend Herschel was supposed to have seen.

The story made life on the moon not terribly different from life in a jungle—what business did cranes have on the moon?—or in one of the fabled levels of purgatory. The flesh is made yellow; even the possibility of life on the moon is made into the ordinary racialized spectacular.

Imaginations stretch out *infinitely,* is the story that we tell about them, proving the inconceivable complexity of each holy brain, the boundlessness our minds are capable of in every millisecond often enough does the work of the eternity formerly known as gods. But sometimes when we lie on purpose, and especially when we do so for fun, our visions stay very close and instead rebuild what's already a home for everyone to live in, but are able to call it something new.

MAGICAL HABITS

At first the word *nostalgia* described sailors, soldiers, and anyone in an exile.[4] *Nostalgia* was a disease not of memory, but of a body that kept acting out strange habits: a complaint for being far from home, even, a common malady. Svetlana Boym distills the seventeenth-century Swiss doctor, Johannes Hofer, who coined the term, when she writes, "Longing for home exhausted the 'vital spirits,' causing nausea, loss of appetite, a disturbance in the lungs, brain inflammation, cardiac arrests, high fever, as well as marasmus and a propensity for suicide."[5] Jerking necks to one side at each pause, as if there was something kept caught in throats that might clear or maybe not; shoulders raising slightly to ears as if caught by surprise or a sudden chill; a snarl recurring for no foe. Then just before the twentieth century solidified the promise that most social problems had ready solutions—and before breaking that promise over the poorest shoulders—there were those that started to write about Jewishness as though it were the nervous effects of a weakness of mind born from ancient wandering. Boym continues, "The spread of nostalgia had to do not only with dislocation in space but also with the changing conception of time. Nostalgia was a historical emotion."[6] If it was a physical malady first and then an accusation of enfeebled culture, then a symptom of history: If I try to pass through it to get to the other side but cannot leave, how to cure it? Or, what would "curing" be? To become someone else?

I try to build a fiction to loosen the pressure in my stomach, the acid and the heat, the sweat across my upper lip. I want the fiction so I can win and never do it again, the cure to end all cures. Each time I promise it's the last time; then I'll have it done, the way all fictions have happened before I get to them. Each time, the promise makes me go further, faster, to get it over sooner, to get to the story I'll tell about how I won, and finally finished. To do it again. And keep winning when I know all the rules and no one else is playing.

Imitating a satiated cat, I lick my fingertips, quickly, one by one, circle my pointed tongue into the space between each nail and plump fingertip, tracing the shape of each, pushing the blunt edges of my nail against my teeth, then following the nail bed, where the texture changes, my mouth slicker and stickier with each pass. Alone, I can be noisy. It's been so long this has been the way that it's started to taste better. I find my rhythm, and like all music it starts with a quiet pulse, and with the time before memory that we keep reaching memory back toward, which just means that before we could see we could hear, which just means we were born with our eyes closed but knew how to sing.

I hear all of it: smacking sounds against the roof and from the sides of my mouth. The abrasive crinkle of the wrapper against the air each time my hand reaches in. That becomes the sound of sneaking, but also of determination and focus. Then, with time, once it's become paste, all the slower, methodical sounds. There's comfort there, and compassion as I make a new heartbeat. I reach furiously into the bag before finishing chewing, and if there's resentment, it's not clear for whom: no one else is there. I have the next handful before I can take a clean, remembering breath.

But if the fiction is going to work, it has to hold all my forgetting.

"This is the last one," I convince myself without arriving at believing and when there are still so many more. I insist, "Just this one. This last one. This one. This one more. Just one. This one more. Just one. One more." If I finish it fast, I will be done and it will be over and I can have a fiction to call home instead of home. Like all fictions, I can know what it looks like, but it cannot see me. I made sure, and listen for steps in the dark just in case.

I start going faster to follow the rhythm, and the way the fiction goes, I'll stop when it's empty. And the way the fiction goes, as empty gets closer, it gets faster. I've said it before and the repetition gently rocks and stings, in turn. I want it all gone and I want a fiction, so I can climb and get more. But in the same instant: if I get more, I will have more, and look like this again, and need it to be gone, but need all of it to be mine, the way a fiction can have our name on it because we were there even if we don't use it. I want it all gone to not think about it, and think instead about another warm, intractable fiction. I want to win even when I can't make out against whom.

I overfill my mouth until it strains to be neat, until I can't stand to be there anymore and I stay, and chew as fast as I can, and reach again. I litter crumbs onto my shirt, wipe a greasy hand against an outer thigh, quickly so no one who isn't there will come in and find me to say what I've been practicing all the while.

I can only be clumsy. It's silly to fight with what I can barely swallow, but right now I'll do it anyway. The problem is in the beginning, looking for something the next mouthful might have.

Someone said the rule of law is fueled by our desire for it, and this is the rule I have: I'll know if I find it. It has to be that way and I'll keep looking. I'll keep needing to know. I'll keep looking. I'll find it and in the meanwhile I'll build a whole world and a warm, confining fiction from a singular need.

I want to ask astronomers if they can trace any shift in the circadian rhythms of the universe to the Internet, or, specifically, to the switch from dial-up to cable DSL connections. Did the Internet slow down galactic expansion because email and smartphones might emit enough electromagnetic waves to keep us all together, the way we keep hoping? It's funny to follow the weather but smirk at astrology. What made it important to decide between the rain and restlessness?—as though a moment (besides that of our annihilation) will come when either finally stops for us.

A day is still a day, the kind that has nothing to do with a clock. But maybe choices can start happening so fast we forget that we chose. I can't say if that's the same as forgetting how to choose, and what would someone have to ask people to remember or to choose, and how long in a generation does it take for everyone to forget one thing together? We've been watching it happen in plain sight.

The last time, she gave me a thin, crooked scarf she thinks she was able to knit for me. Today she can't remember my name. Her hands had the shakes by then; I'm surprised she could hold the needles long enough to make a scarf, even one this short. She repeats, Sólo quiero trabajar, until it's barely more than the murmur of a song. She's been my guardian angel for more than ten years when I realize she was trying to tell me that work—it could be any kind of work, it takes me a lifetime to learn—is a way of being brave even when you don't know who you are, or what name to use, without waiting for the right moment, a revelation, inside or outside your mind.

All those years she knit in a house surrounded by so many ways to wait for what no one was willing to say, with pictures on the wall, and a postcard in the nightstand. She read it to me each time and would still be reading it if she were there and I were visiting.

One of her friends in the house was named Pera. Pera had a girlish crush on Guillermo, who couldn't hear well but could still pull his legs through his own pants in the morning, which in that house really did mean something. Guillermo let Pera listen to him talk about the car he had when he was seventeen, about his first wife, Gabriela's laugh, and, when he turned somber from missing her laugh, he would describe what it felt like to wake up again, sometimes what it felt like to wake up with her after a lifetime together of waking up. I wanted to know what she was going to say. She had the most vivid dreams, and sometimes nightmares that she believed, and I would have to remind her that whatever upsetting thing hadn't happened. Pera asked him if he'd ever wanted to be a poet. Gabriela visited him once, and they spoke like old friends in half sentences and long, winsome pauses. She was the only person he could hear without straining, without leaning forward. She wasn't visiting that day, but she told me about Gabriela's visit before reaching into the nightstand for the postcard.

Te la he leido? No, Abue. She had, many times. Mira. Me la mandó tu abuelo.

The front of the postcard was a photograph of a boy handing a girl a rose, tinted pink like their cheeks. They sat on a park bench. On the back of the postcard, in a strong, slanted hand: Estrellita. Ya mero regreso para darte todas las rosas que tanto te mereces. El trabajo me anda llendo bien. Parece que sólo otros pocos meses más. Ya verás, se pasará el tiempo de un día para otro. Abrázame a los chamacos. Los amo y los adoro a todos. Siempre tuyo, Marcos. He—a violent and abusive alcoholic—had left when my mom was two. When he died, another family he'd made laid him to rest. I took the scarf home.

I stopped looking for all the photographs to lay them next to each other and confuse all our faces, to see if sometimes it matters and other times it doesn't matter who's who. I lost a little of my old love for order moving between all these coasts; I won't ask out of the blue to start again now, but another part of me wants to be ready in case I run out of history. The point is that I want to be ready if one day I can't find any more. I want to be ready to be surprised even if I suspect I'm going to have to be nostalgic about someone before I can love them. I really don't know how it will work. But when the shock comes, what or who will convince me not to retrace my steps?

The problem with photographs is simple and obvious, and it's this: we can keep them and they pretend to keep us back. Thomas Wedgwood, the story goes, was on a boating trip when, after months of trying, he finally caught light on paper. It took decades to solve the next problem, how to make the marks stay. Ever since, we've been married to the promise of keeping what we don't yet understand by recording its shadow and naming it. It's a curious investment, sometimes hopeful, sometimes less so. Either we don't want to miss anything, or we're convinced that's all we do. Once light had a speed it was harder to believe we wouldn't fall behind if we blinked. That's what archives were for at first, not for keeping history safe but for making sure we kept up with time.

The graybeards of history wear their wisdom like sobriety, but historians have it all wrong: nothing has ever been waiting for us to find it or to figure it out. Holiness must lie elsewhere than in being lost or found, if we are the ones looking. Any archive can be for hiding and for keeping and maybe some reasons are good enough. It could be like Hide and Keep, with room for dancing. There are histories we need, and yet I want to ask if there's some rest in what's going to be missing, because something will be, because that's what makes time holy, because time needs to be a prism if we are all going to be here.

It is only heresy if we say so (it is only heresy, *if we say so!*).

Free will is a terrible inheritance and already a misnomer for the small, quiet space from which world-making begins and through which it is contained. Free of bodies? Free of history? Free of responsibility? Free of limits? What monstrous race of people could believe in it wholesale? Some of our own. Our choices are not "free" of much, but they are ours as soon as we make them. My dear friend's mom taught me that. They are ours in that we have to live with them, we become enmeshed in them just as we're enmeshed in so much else. They are ours, however tenderly, and bend us toward freedom or unfreedom, even if it can also be unclear in a moment which is which. Critique can recognize an aftermath.

History—like memory and all other stories—can be a prison house, or a storehouse, or a workshop, or a bad movie, or a treasure trove, or a love story, or a tedious task, and choosing which one means you're going to have a certain kind of day. It's also a postcard my grandmother kept in her nightstand even after she couldn't tell the difference between day and night and standing and sitting and laying down. Or it's what stays between me and my sister and the school portraits from the early nineties she kept on the walls of the nursing home where I visited her in Guadalajara those last years, after many years have passed in which I don't see her or anyone in my family. All six of her grandchildren, framed and kept safe where she could find them, those last years with the postcard in the dresser. She couldn't always tell, Are you Mónica or María? On any given day, to her, it also didn't matter. One of us was there.

We keep photographs (like postcards) in mind as in drawers and the danger is that we stay with them. That's why we love them immediately and without question. It's easy to be seduced by stillness as though it's safety. So many centuries trying to add up to the number one, we disremembered our homes can be scattered like nomads. They remind us how far they can be from one another and from us, how our stories mean we're larger than our bodies even though they may lead us back to them. But how to tell whether a memory is keeping me company or gripping my hand? Should we try to let go—even before deciding whether to leave behind or keep stories about machines, science, coffins for light, traces of history, or God?

I've watched all the videos that got lost between Chicago and Florida and Chicago and all the coasts and wherever I might move next when I get restless or another job. And if I watched them all over again again, I'd always be able to find something I don't remember. The truth is, I have a terrible memory; that's likely how the repetition game got started. But if I watched them all, I might Hide and Keep all those treasured details, what literature has been stretching to find language for since before Dickens described dirt under lawyers' feet. Habits are habits: I've even read social theorists and psychologists to make sure. But here's my question: what to do since the Protestant work ethic never had me in mind? If work can be a way to be brave, a way to reject pure mechanism, enough work might bring me to the felt difference between horizons, asymptotes, and vanishing points—or else lay me at their feet peacefully, to wash over me like the tides turning.

I paid to have a Betamax tape transferred to a DVD some years ago. Everything but the part in our Palos Hills living room remains and plays back with perfect sound and crystal-clear picture, as though it were 1987, as though the reporter and cameraman had just left, with me wearing the silk lilac dress and pigtails that skimmed my shoulders while I answered the reporter's questions about my favorite food at the restaurants—garnachas . . . y quesadillas—smoothing hair out of my face like she taught me. Para que se te vea la cara, she said so many times, y no parescas bruja. If only she could see how long (and blue) my hair has lately been and I could ask her whether she thought maybe there are some good witches too.

Without the inevitable vagaries of the technologies we put our leftover faith in, I could have heard what he sounded like in the time before it would feel important to remember. It's not exactly what I wanted, but some kind of proof of a time when I didn't need to either remember or play a game to forget will have to be good enough.

I've wanted to pile it all up in a pile to see who is taller: me or the photographs. (The photographs.) Me or all the history. (The history.) Me or capitalism's founding myths, which were about progress in exactly this sense: that there were cannibals on darker continents that needed to be tamed with guns in civilization's name. The same ones that make it easy for my parents to sell tacos to take me across oceans in the tradition of money looking for its reason, the same tacos that feed anyone's hunger and that kept me from taking out student loans. There really is nothing I am not invulnerable to. You too.

After that, the stories we hold and devour like addictions might hide us from asking how we learned to be this insatiable, how to hold many hungers in abeyance for long enough to ask which is which kind of inheritance, long enough to choose which to feed, which to starve. Those might end (it could be a relief) with an utterance which, among other things, is the beginning of so much pain: "It's mine." A demarcation, a quiet release ("that other is not mine"). And even so, two short beats, just one spondee, could take a lifetime to find and earn and could also be a beginning if we say it right, if we find and keep habits to surrender to one another, if we say it like surrender, writing as though it matters that one day you might be given the chance—can you remember it's always an honor? can you remember it's always taken work especially when it's messy (it's mostly always messy)?—to hold more than the singular story in your palm when we shake hands. If we find and keep the habits to make ourselves safe for others to surrender to. It's already happened, from another and even the most material vantage. I'm breathing this broken air in broken time with you.

There is so much ordinary magic to be found in dispelling modernity's myths and finding better spells. *Mine* without sovereignty or possession. One suspended moment in an onrush, the sound and space and dimension into which even that sound disappears.

What are you doing here? I have this to give. A vanishing point where history is pivoting. Offerings as though we are the horizon.

SEPTEMBER 2013 *Brooklyn, Munsee-Lenape homelands*
REVISED OCTOBER 2019 *Philadelphia, Lenni-Lenape homelands*

8:58 PM

Hi Monica, How r u? We think of u often and hope all is well. We are finally cleaning the garage and found 3 big yearbooks from St Andrews school and a photo album from Disneyland 1996—what would u like us to do with them?

Big hugs, S and S

THERE IS NO WAY TO STOP except to say this particular book is over now. That's what it means to be in the midst of a habit, even the habit of aiming toward a slice, however slim, of space between the steps of a habit. And even if you can find it, the habit might yet go on.

Thank you, reader. My very first thanks is to you and here is why: There are many flavors of loneliness, and one of them is when you don't know what you're doing, and you're doing it anyway. There's nothing in particular to talk about with anyone. What would you say? I tinker with some sentences, some paragraphs; I have some notions; I don't know for what and I don't much know why. So over the long stretch of time when I was with the pages that are now this book, I was that kind of lonely. Thank you, dear reader, not for relieving that loneliness as though now we are friends, but for relieving that loneliness in that you exist as this book's reader because I am no longer that kind of lonely, at least not about this book. This book exists, and so I do not have to be lonely with it because I do not have to be with it not knowing what it is. Another quiet form of freedom is finishing something in the incremental, incomplete ways that there are to finish—even if the press deadline did just as much of the finishing as me. The part I'll do is let go.

And in all this not-stopping—except that this book is over now—that will continue after the book is there with you, there would have been no way of being something other than lonely without very many kind and beloved hearts.

My adored college roommates (Alex, Ana, Chondita, Deena, Jen, Sarah) have been a North Star for me as long as they've been with me. It is impossible to overstate what their ambition, love, humor, and intellect meant to me and meant for me. It's in keeping with the tenacity with which we approach a day that some of those relations have frayed, so dedicated are we each to the thick, delicious lives we've built.

The Kuumba+ fam (Ashley, Barry, Danielle, Frances, Jason, Jason, Jason, Jessica, Jessica, Johanna, Jorge, Kamala, Kelley, Lindsay, Maleka, Marcel, Melanie, Michaela, Mulk, Okwui, Padmini, Quincy, Savannah, Scott, Sheldon, Tom, and legions more) has been part of my chosen family since I knew that I might also choose one. We didn't have a pact, but I'm sincerely moved by how we've each kept Kuumba's mission: to try and leave the places we pass through better than we found them.

There are some places, like Princeton, where it was not obvious to me that I would find a friend. And, first as a graduate student (Carolyn, David, Najam), then while at the Society of Fellows (Ale, Ava, Bernadette, Catherine, Justin, Laurel, Mary, Nijah, Stefan, Tala), and now as a faculty member (Autumn, Christina, Dan-el, Irene, Josh, Kinohi, Paul, Russ), in fact Princeton has gifted me friendships in heaps. Ale and his no-punches-pulled notes pushed a draft through at a crucial moment to its more final stages. Through a shared Dropbox folder, Carolyn has been this book's doula for almost the entire time I didn't know what I was doing. I'm going to unshare it with you now, horse friend, but only because there are other shared folders.

At UC Berkeley in graduate school part two, we made a little village of singing and eating alongside the other graduate school rituals. I love you, Irene, Sasha, Lili, Aaron, Gina, Sarah, Megan. A special shout to Megan, who read this book a zillion years ago. Another special shout to Sasha for being my basketball-watching, life-troubleshooting, did-you-make-sure-to-eat text go-to. And to Sarah, now my fellow garden-level dweller: what a time, what a thing.

In the two years I spent in Durham on a postdoc, I was lucky to find some fellow travelers. I am so thankful that we met and decided to become writing buddies, Ashley; so thankful for nacho traditions, Liz and Jecca and Marisol; and for the space to stay mystical, China. It is an extra and outlandish kind of treat and blessing, Liz, to work with you on this book.

I finished this book in the middle of the COVID-19 pandemic, a stretch of time that grew its own rituals of sustaining intimacy. It feels important to mark with eternal high-fives the care of so many overlapping and expanding networks: Horror Movie Club, the trivia team known as Medicare for All (Total Landscaping Co.), OG SOF, Music League(s), Kuumba Zooms, and each of their lively Whats App threads, much more actual than virtual. There is no way to write toward a more desirable future without knowing in your bones it's already tucked into here, just waiting to be unfurled.

I have a sprawling team of mentors without whom I would be even more of a wanderer:

Thank you, Dirk, for reading everything I ever asked you to read, including this one, for being cool with my extreme frankness, and for letting me cry when I needed exactly and only that too. And for not really changing at all in your way with me, from when I was just out of college and obnoxiously over-confident to now, when I hope to be at least a little less obnoxious.

Thank you, Priscilla, for every bit of honesty and compassion, and for becoming my friend.

Thank you, Susan, for introducing me in a new way to the outer limits of the joys in this kind of lifework.

Thank you, Elisa, for every time you asked me to send you the revisions again, and for every way you showed me what mentorship could be, and that it was possible to enjoy being a woman who set boundaries with grace. So many of the ways I adopted to help me thrive I learned from you.

Thank you, Stephen, for investing in me from that first seminar on "servility" 'til now. It's only in finishing this book that I realized just how much it is marked by thinking with you.

Thank you, Tamsen, for letting me mourn with you the day Prince died, and for being unflinchingly on my team since then.

Thank you, Anna, for dinners and real talk and the space to imagine a whole other way things could be.

Thank you, Rachael, for every conversation and very real laugh.

Thank you, Kyla, for the clutch fuzzy socks and always-loving enthusiasm.

Thank you, Reg, for the wide-open perspective of your seemingly unflappable sanity.

Thank you, Judith, for being so deeply wise and smart and kind. I treasure our teas.

Thank you, Michael, for offering key insights exactly when I need them, and for always being willing to hash something out, no matter how small.

Thank you, Eduardo, for your warmth, steadfast support, and example.

Thank you, Bill and Simon, for being dedicated department chairs for untenured folks.

I also want to thank Andrea Volpe, who was a lecturer in the History and Literature program at Harvard and who was assigned as my thesis advisor. I lost touch with her many moons ago, but it was only her tenacious attention to my writing that made sure I wrote something leaps and bounds better than I would have otherwise. And, too, as someone who has adjuncted at several institutions, I want to acknowledge how much crucial work of all kinds people in precarious job conditions do at universities, in ever-worsening conditions and with fewer and fewer resources. Our institutions owe them all much more stability and dignity, and much more than stability and dignity.

In many obvious senses, I would not have written this book without my family. But if it might seem like a meager form of appreciation, for me it really is the opposite: thank you for the space to figure out which were going to be my ways, even as you've all had very many other ideas.

Last, I'd like to acknowledge some of the habits I've needed for this book: ignoring the loud bar under my apartment in Crown Heights; early Sia; acupuncture; all of Prince, but especially "Erotic City" and "Adore"; the view when working on the balcony of my last apartment in Oakland; Amy Winehouse, "Tears Dry on Their Own"; fizzy water, especially black cherry and lime flavors; Belanova; sitting still and quietly for hours on hours; astrology; Adele, *19*; sleep hypnosis podcasts; Arvo Pärt; therapy; Netflix stand-up specials; Beres Hammond, "Sweet Lies"; dining hall breakfast; Patty Griffin, "Let Him Fly"; ignoring when the neighbor's kids fight or dribble basketballs indoors in Philly; Jackson 5, "Who's Lovin' You"; enjoying packing up so many apartments; D'Angelo; restorative yoga; Julieta Venegas, "Limón y Sal"; transcendental meditation; Joni Mitchell, "River"; rooibos tea; early Madonna; Trader Joe's snacks, especially elote corn chip dippers; Michael Kiwanuka; Sam Cooke; egg salad with red onion; kombucha, all flavors; Stevie Wonder; barre class; Brazilian Girls, "Me Gusta Cuando Callas"; grocery store sushi; bone broth; Phil Collins; taro milk tea with boba; Peter Cetera; and red bean bun.

PREFACE

1 Boym, *The Future of Nostalgia*, 8.
2 Nicola Miller in Biagini et al., "Interchange," 471.
3 Gómez, *Manifest Destinies*, 17.
4 See Molina, *How Race Is Made*; and López, *White by Law*.
5 Figueroa-Vásquez, *Decolonizing Diasporas*, 11.
6 It is not without a sense of historical irony that one of the best-known sites of Chicano mobilizing and protest against the City of Chicago happened at Benito Juárez High School on the lower west side of Chicago. See Marroquin, "Youth as Engaged Cultural Workers."
7 For essays on the ways indigenous communities throughout Mexico worked both against and within Juárez's liberal, consolidating reforms, see Ohmstede, *Los pueblos indios*.
8 In *The Transit of Empire*, Jodi Byrd borrows the term *arrivant* from poet Kamau Brathwaite to theorize horizontally among indigenous peoples and racialized peoples and as an attempt to signal the ongoing displacements of settler colonialism.
9 Khanna, *The Visceral Logics of Decolonization*, 1.
10 In their important article, "Decolonization Is Not a Metaphor," Eve Tuck and K. Wayne Yang "remind readers what is unsettling about decolonization," which "brings about the repatriation of Indigenous land and life" (1). The article enumerates the ways in which making decolonization into a metaphor, even a critical one, even one oriented toward social justice ends, plays into the production of what they term "settler moves to innocence" (1). Taking their provocation seriously, in this preface I avoid using the term as a metaphor, and write about other motivations and intellectual practices as working "toward decolonization."
11 I'm inspired here and elsewhere by the ana-grammatical insights of Black feminism as related by Christina Sharpe in *In the Wake*.
12 Combahee River Collective, "The Combahee River Collective Statement," 19.
13 Paul Bloom distinguishes between cognitive and emotional empathy in *Against Empathy*. These are helpful categories. I would suggest, too, that there might be a way to think of each of these as embedded in the histories by which some are more and less easily empathizable, in any register.
14 Serpell, "The Banality of Empathy."
15 Holland, "When Characters Lack Character."
16 Seremetakis, *Sensing the Everyday*, 5.

17 As I've written these sections, I've often thought of the moment in the intro-
    duction to *Touching Feeling* when Eve Sedgwick describes the trouble and risks
    of seeking to write "nondualistically": "I've always assumed that the most
    useful work of this sort is the likeliest to occur near the boundary of what a
    writer can't figure out how to say readily, never mind prescribe to others: in
    the Jacoblike wrestling—or t'ai chi, as it may be—that confounds agency with
    passivity, the self with the book and the world, the ends of the work with its
    means, and, maybe most alarmingly, intelligence with stupidity" (2). She cites
    her stubbornness as related to being a Taurus. Alas, my own is Cancerian.
18 I am ever thankful for the generous thinking and work of Eli Meyerhoff, Nick
    Mitchell, and other critical university studies scholars.

1. THE SYNTHESIS PROBLEM

1 Kathleen Stewart's remarkable attention to the ordinary as intensities made
   available through critical description kept me sane in my own making out of
   the ordinary in these essays. Stewart, *Ordinary Affects.*
2 Reading Sianne Ngai on the gimmick clarified why I thought this was the right
   and ironic question to ask here, and why we need and want splotches. S. Ngai,
   "Theory of the Gimmick."
3 The cardiovascular system of these essays aligns best with Antonio Viego's vision for multicultural, antiracist Lacanian subjects, split and so unmanageable
   either by state projects or by the attendant aesthetic projects that make ethnic
   subjects palatable. Viego, *Dead Subjects.*
4 Everything I know about color, I learned from Nicholas Gaskill. Gaskill,
   Chromographia.
5 Huerta, "What's Mine"; Mensel, "'Kodakers Lying in Wait.'"
6 Scholars like Tao Leigh Goffe and Kyla Wazana Tompkins have done important work to expand the questions and insights that can be gained through
   studying foodways.
7 I submitted "The Burrito Dream: Authenticity and Cultural Hybridity in Mexican Restaurants in Late-Twentieth-Century Chicago" to the Committee on
   Degrees in History and Literature in partial fulfillment of the requirements for
   the degree of bachelor of arts with honors at Harvard College, in Cambridge,
   Massachusetts, on February 28, 2003. If you search for it on HOLLIS, Harvard's
   online library catalog, it may help to have the HOLLIS ID# 990095161050203941.
8 For an extended series of studies on this moment in world-making, see Flores,
   Aparicio, Mora-Torres, and Torres, *The Mexican Revolution in Chicago*; and *Historic City: The Settlement of Chicago,* commissioned by the City of Chicago
   Department of Development and Planning. The latter publication commu-
   nicates the explicit goal of tracing the "ethnic" immigration into the city of
   Chicago.
9 "The war [World War I] stimulated the migration and importation of Mexican labor into Chicago for the first time; their numbers equaled or surpassed

the increase of black workers, and Mexicans suggest a provocative comparison group with blacks." Pinderhughes, *Race and Ethnicity in Chicago Politics*, 17–18.

10 For a more contemporary version of this synthesis, see Valerio-Jiménez, Vaquera-Vásquez, and Fox, introduction; and Nicholas De Genova's theorization of "Mexican Chicago" in *Working the Boundaries*.

In the excerpted and edited sections of my senior thesis, I've tried to balance presenting a sense of the thesis itself while updating some of the citations to link to the ways scholarship has changed since the moment of its writing. For example, I then used the frame of diaspora rather than that of immigration because, in the early 2000s, scholarship about Mexican Americans seemed to me limited by the strictures of an implicit model in which labor markets drove immigration and so also the frame of analysis. Since then, so much work in Latina/o/x studies has been reoriented. For example, the editors of *The Latina/o Studies Reader* write, "Scholars working on the Chicana/o, Mexicana/o Midwesterners in particular point out that perspectives on the US Southwest as an occupied ancestral homeland do not enter into Chicana/o-Mexicana/o narrative self-representations in the Midwest to the extent that diasporic and immigrant perspectives do, bringing Chicanas/os and Mexicanas/os into closer alignment with the diasporic imaginations of other Latina/o groups, although the former continue to comprise the majority among Latinas/os." Valerio-Jiménez, Vaquera-Vásquez, and Fox, introduction, 17.

11 Lindberg, *Passport's Guide*, 349. The first permanent settlement of Mexicans in Chicago dates to 1900. All information taken from the series of maps presented for each decade from 1870 to 1950 in *Historic City*.

12 For a careful and illuminating study of the creation of the idea of "illegal aliens" through migration, please see Lew-Williams, *The Chinese Must Go*.

13 Briggs, *Mexican Migration*, 6.

14 "Los Mexicanos en Chicago."

15 The year 1930 also saw over 850,000 immigrants enter Chicago's city limits, especially Italians, Lithuanians, Poles, and Mexicans. Only Mexicans were targeted for massive deportations.

16 Lindberg, *Passport's Guide*, 351.

17 Briggs, *Mexican Migration*, 6.

18 Lindberg, *Passport's Guide*, 352; Rosales, "Fighting the Peace."

19 George Sánchez's canonical study of Mexican Americans in Los Angeles gives a deep cultural history of this kind of community organizing and its various shades of political allegiances. Sánchez, *Becoming Mexican American*.

20 "The discordant voices of 1,000 community residents were heard outside the offices of the Board of Education the day of the vote, until the members caved into the tremendous political pressure and agreed to build the spacious Benito Juárez High School, which was designed by a Mexican architect named Ramirez Vazquez. Juárez . . . offers bilingual education." Lindberg, *Passport's Guide*, 352.

21 "Los Mexicanos en Chicago," 2. For narratives of Chicano mobilization during

the 1960s and 1970s, see Muñoz, *Youth, Identity, Power*; Gómez-Quiñones, *Chicano Politics*, especially chapter 3. José Angel Gutiérrez's *The Making of a Chicano Militant* is an autobiography that focuses on Raza Unida Party.

22 Current research by Mae Ngai demonstrates that, contrary to the myth of America as a "nation of immigrants," the wave of immigration at the turn of the century from countries like Ireland and Poland (i.e., those groups that became "white ethnic") were the exception in US history in the sense that the conditions into which they migrated were structurally beneficial to them in a way that has not been the case for any other series of migrations. Mae M. Ngai, "A Nation of Immigrants."

23 Jones-Correa, *Between Two Nations*.

24 Jones-Correa, *Between Two Nations*, chapter 7.

2. FABULATION

1 For a transnational reexamination of Cristeros, see Young, *Mexican Exodus*.

2 Theoretical physicist and Black feminist theorist Chanda Prescod-Weinstein has made the cosmos legible to me in a new way, offering its knowledges as another mode through which to make visions for justice real. I am indebted to her brilliant work across multiple fields. Prescod-Weinstein, *The Disordered Cosmos*.

3 Alatorre Huerta, *Salvador Huerta Gutiérrez*, 12.

4 Alatorre Huerta, *Salvador Huerta Gutiérrez*, 9.

5 Alatorre Huerta, *Salvador Huerta Gutiérrez*, 9.

6 For an excellent discussion of the migration routes of Cristeros, see Young, "Cristero Diaspora."

7 Kelly and Satola, "The Right to Be Forgotten."

8 "El vitral del Santuario de los Mártires de Guadalajara: una obra que desborda fe, arte e ingeniería," *Religion en Libertad*, March 2, 2019, https://www.religion enlibertad.com/america_latina/889709979/El-vitral-del-Santuario-de-los -Martires-de-Guadalajara-una-obra-maestra-de-fe-arte-e-ingenieria.html.

9 Mariana Coronado Mendoza, "Celebran más de 10 mil fieles la primera misa en el Santuario de los Mártires," *Milenio*, November 23, 2015, https://www.milenio .com/estados/celebran-10-mil-fieles-misa-santuario-martires.

10 The essays in *Mexican American Religions: Spirituality, Activism, and Culture* help connect my engagement with my family's Mexican Catholic practices to those of Mexican Americans of other contexts and faiths. Espinosa and García, *Mexican American Religions*.

3. DISCIPLINES AND DISCIPLES

1 Biltoft, "Against Scholarly Enclosures."

2 Park, "Money, Mortgages, and the Conquest of America."

3 Saidiya Hartman's thinking about archives has been important to my and so many others' thinking and writing (see *Lose Your Mother*). I owe a debt here, too, to Christina Sharpe's *In the Wake*.

4 Duncan, "The Literature of Alchemy."

5 Ginzburg, *Myths, Emblems, Clues.*

6 Salvador's Restaurantes Mexicanos menu, c. 1983, Chicago; author's personal collection.

7 Salvador's Restaurantes Mexicanos menu, c. 1983.

8 Salvador's Restaurantes Mexicanos menu, c. 1983.

9 Salvador's Restaurantes Mexicanos menu, c. 1983.

10 Salvador's Restaurantes Mexicanos menu, c. 1983.

11 Salvador's Restaurantes Mexicanos menu, c. 1983.

12 Salvador Huerta, letter to author, 2002.

13 Huerta, letter to author, 2002.

14 Huerta, letter to author, 2002.

15 Salvador's Restaurantes Mexicanos menu, c. 1987, Chicago; author's personal collection.

16 For Eduardo Cadava and Paola Cortés-Rocca, it's precisely the "un-selfing" function of a photograph from which its loving caress arises. Cadava and Cortés-Rocca, "Notes on Love and Photography."

4. APHORISM AS A PROMISE

1 Phelan, *Unmarked.*

2 Baldwin, "Stranger in the Village."

3 Leticia Alvarado's work thinking with artists who turn away from the strictures of communicating ethnic pride or redemption has been crucial to understanding my own choices here in conversation with other Latinx artists and cultural producers. Alvarado, *Abject Performances.*

5. HEARTBREAK AS PRAXIS

1 Edwards, "Objects of Affect."

2 Doane, *Emergence of Cinematic Time.*

3 Daniel Gutiérrez, interview by author, September 28, 2002, Chicago.

4 María Eugenia Cotera lays out some of the historical particularities of belonging/unbelonging for Latinxs in the Midwest in the context of the Museo del Norte in Detroit. Cotera, "El Museo del Norte."

5 Gutiérrez, interview.

6 Gutiérrez, interview.

7 Part of Gutiérrez's life in Chicago was serving as a medic in the American army for two years; he graduated in 1965 and was drafted in 1966 along with two other brothers: "We were gone for two years. Until 1968. My father and my mother I think had a rough time by themselves. Only my older brother wasn't drafted. So he was the one that stayed with my parents. . . . We came back. . . . We got lucky." Gutiérrez, interview.

8 Gutiérrez, interview.

9 Nuevo León Restaurant menu, c. 1990, Chicago; author's personal collection.

10 Nuevo León Restaurant menu, c. 1990.

11 The additional wrinkle is that none of these people are Native in that they do not identify as affiliated with any peoples indigenous to the Americas. Each is participating in distinct ways with settler colonial formations.

12 Holmes, "The Stereoscope and the Stereograph."

13 hooks, *All about Love*.

14 Steedman, *Dust*.

15 Bloch, "The Wolf in the Dog."

16 I've been deeply inspired by the multiple kinds of work Alexis Pauline Gumbs has been doing on and with Black Feminist Breath, in multiple genres of writing, workshops, and collages. For one of her early articulations, see Gumbs, "That Transformative Dark Thing." In *Dub: Finding Ceremony*, Gumbs writes, "This project is an artifact and tool for breath retraining and interspecies ancestral listening. It is structured to ask, what if you could breathe like whales who sing underwater and recycle air to sing again before coming up for air? What if you could breathe like coral from a multitude of simultaneous openings connected to one source built upon the bones of all your dead? . . . When you think it's time to come up for air, go deeper. When you think your heart will break, stay there, stay with it. But at the same time, when you think you gotta hold onto something (like who you think you are), let go." So much of this book takes this invitation with utter seriousness. Gumbs, *Dub*, xiii.

17 Parisi, Paterson, and Archer, "Haptic Media Studies."

6. WHETHER WISDOM

1 For an important history of Spanish in the United States and to give context for how it is that English comes to predominate, see Lozano, *An American Language*.

7. BEFORE AND AFTER

1 The writing I do here with photographs would have been less brave without Roland Barthes's *Camera Lucida*.

2 Ava Shirazi's theories of materiality and cultural history of ancient Greek mirrors have been deeply informative to my thinking about mirrors here. Shirazi, "The Mirror and the Senses."

3 I am indebted to the essays in Elspeth H. Brown and Thy Phu's *Feeling Photography* and to their lucid introduction, which lays out an intellectual history for the omission of thinking about the feelings inspired by looking at and thinking with photographs.

4 Rick Bayless was selected as the Best New Chef of 1988 by *Food and Wine*; in 1991, the James Beard Foundation voted him Best American Chef: Midwest; and in 1995 he won both the James Beard Foundation's National Chef of the Year award and the International Association of Culinary Professional's Chef

of the Year award. Frontera Grill was also chosen by Patricia Wells at the *International Herald Tribune* as one of the best casual restaurants in the world.

5   Frontera Grill menu, c. 1987, Chicago; author's personal collection.
6   This is the version of the world where someone else's pain is understood to make the food taste better.
7   Phil Vettel, "A Dazzling Feast of Flavors," *Chicago Tribune*, April 25, 2001.
8   Vettel, "A Dazzling Feast."
9   Phil Vettel, "Former Topolobampo Chef Hits Home Run," *Chicago Tribune*, November 1, 2000.
10 Geno Bahena, interview by author, September 28, 2002, Chicago.
11 Bahena, interview.
12 Ixcapuzalco Restaurant menu, c. 1995, Chicago; author's personal collection.
13 Ixcapuzalco Restaurant menu, c. 1995.
14 Ixcapuzalco Restaurant menu, c. 1995.
15 Vettel, "Former Topolobampo Chef."
16 Bayless's employment serving as social capital is not limited to Bahena. The *Chicago Tribune* recommends Satkoff's Salpicón Restaurant, whose menu echoes Bayless's contemporary Mexican menu. In praising Satkoff, the article states, "Chef Priscila Satkoff got her start cooking under Rick Bayless at the much-lauded Frontera Grill/Topolobampo, but we think the student has become the master." Greg Schlegel, "Neato Burritos, Top Tacos: Top 5 Mexican," *Chicago Tribune*, April 25, 2001.

2006

1   It was more like eight.
2   Hiram Walker Liqueurs, founded in 1858, now part of Pernod Ricard, a French company.

8. WHEN COURTS OF LOVE HAVE CASH REGISTERS

1   Goodrich, *Law in the Courts of Love*.

9. AUCTIONS

1   Fred Farrar, "Chinese Here Keep Ancient Culture Alive," *Chicago Tribune*, November 2, 1961.
2   Farrar, "Chinese Here."
3   Farrar, "Chinese Here."
4   Farrar, "Chinese Here."
5   As one Massachusetts judge would find out in 2006, when asked to decide whether a burrito qualified as a sandwich. He decided against the Panera Bread Company's contentions that a burrito was the same thing in principle and structure as a sandwich.
6   Fred Leavitt, "A Bruising Rodeo Starring the Rough Riders of Chicago's Mexican Colony," *Chicago Tribune Magazine*, October 5, 1962.

7 Leavitt, "A Bruising Rodeo."

8 Leavitt, "A Bruising Rodeo."

9 Leavitt, "A Bruising Rodeo."

10 George Estep, "Untitled," *Chicago Tribune*, January 16, 1977.

11 Articles that deal with undocumented immigration during this time period continue to be printed by Chicago newspapers, however. As late as 1981, Howard A. Tyner described "our vulnerable illegal aliens" as predominantly Mexican in the *Chicago Tribune*. A similar article from 1977 illustrates a perception of the cycle of illegal immigration in Chicago as a particularly Mexican problem. Howard A. Tyner, "Our Vulnerable Illegal Aliens," *Chicago Tribune*, April 29, 1981; David Jackson, "500,000 Illegal Aliens Live, Work in Chicago," *Daily News*, August 13–14, 1977.

12 Estep, "Untitled."

13 Estep, "Untitled."

14 Estep, "Untitled."

15 Estep, "Untitled."

10. UNCERTAINTY AND BATHING

1 "Todo el trabajo de la razón humana tiende a la eliminación del segundo término. *Lo otro no existe*: tal es la fe racional, la incurable creencia de la razón humana. Identidad = realidad, como si, a fin de cuentas, todo hubiera de ser, absoluta y necesariamente, uno y lo mismo. Pero *lo otro* no se deja eliminar: subsiste, persiste; es el hueso duro de roer en que la razón se deja los dientes . . . como si dijéramos en la incurable *otredad* que padece lo *uno*." A. Machado "Juan de Mairena—Sentencias, donaires, apuntes y recuerdos de un profesor apórifo," 1917; emphasis in original.

2 William Grimes, "Restaurants: The Empire That Guacamole Built," *New York Times*, September 20, 2000.

3 Grimes, "Restaurants."

4 Darwin, *Expression of the Emotions*; Prodger, *Darwin's Camera*.

5 Grosz, *Becoming Undone*.

11. AFTER HYPERVIGILANCE

1 S. Ngai, *Ugly Feelings*.

2 Robinson, *Black Marxism*, 106–9.

3 Jennifer Miller, Middle English seminar, fall 2008, University of California, Berkeley.

4 Moten, "Poetics of Violence."

5 "Cinder," in Stewart, *Cinder*, 155.

12. CHOREOGRAPHY

1 Locke, *The Moon Hoax*, 37; this is a reprint of the original 1835 issue, as quoted in Vida, "The 'Great Moon Hoax.'"

2 Vida, "The 'Great Moon Hoax,'" 432.

3 Poe, "Richard Adams Locke," 134; Phineas Taylor Barnum, *Humbugs of the World* (New York: Carleton, 1866), 193; both as quoted in Vida, "The 'Great Moon Hoax,'" 436.
4 Goodman, "'Uncertain Disease.'"
5 Boym, *The Future of Nostalgia*, 3.
6 Boym, *The Future of Nostalgia*, 7.

ARCHIVAL SOURCES

Frontera Grill menu, c. 1987, Chicago. Author's personal collection.
Ixcapuzalco Restaurant menu, c. 1995, Chicago. Author's personal collection.
Nuevo León Restaurant menu, c. 1990, Chicago. Author's personal collection.
Salvador's Restaurantes Mexicanos menu, c. 1982, Chicago. Author's personal collection.
Salvador's Restaurantes Mexicanos menu, c. 1983, Chicago. Author's personal collection.
Salvador's Restaurantes Mexicanos menu, c. 1987, Chicago. Author's personal collection.
Salvador's Restaurantes Mexicanos menu, c. 1993, Chicago. Author's personal collection.

INTERVIEWS AND CORRESPONDENCE

Geno Bahena, interview by author, September 28, 2002, Chicago.
Daniel Gutiérrez, interview by author, September 28, 2002, Chicago.
Salvador Huerta, letter to author, 2002.

SECONDARY SOURCES

Alatorre Huerta, María Guadalupe, ed. *Salvador Huerta Gutiérrez: Recuerdos de Familia.* Tlaquepaque, Mexico: Ediciones Católicas de Guadalajara, 2005.
Alvarado, Leticia. *Abject Performances: Aesthetic Strategies in Latino Cultural Production.* Durham, NC: Duke University Press, 2018.
Baldwin, James. "Stranger in the Village." In *Notes of a Native Son*, 159–75. 1955; Boston: Beacon Press, 2012.
Barthes, Roland. *Camera Lucida: Reflections on Photography.* Translated by Richard Howard. New York: Farrar, Straus and Giroux, 1981.
Bennett, Jane. *The Enchantment of Modern Life: Attachments, Crossings, and Ethics.* Princeton, NJ: Princeton University Press, 2001.
Biagini, Eugenio F., David W. Blight, Carolyn P. Boyd, Richard Carwardine, Kevin K. Gaines, Vinay Lal, Nicola Miller, Jörg Nagler, Jay Sexton, Adam I. P. Smith, and Odd Arne Westad. "Interchange: The Global Lincoln." *Journal of American History* 96, no. 2 (2009): 462–99.

Biltoft, C. N. "Against Scholarly Enclosures: Reconsidering the Art and Economics of Review." *Capitalism: A Journal of History and Economics* 1, no. 1 (2019): 231–36.

Bloch, R. Howard. "The Wolf in the Dog: Animal Fables and State Formation." *differences* 15, no. 1 (2004): 69–83.

Bloom, Paul. *Against Empathy: The Case for Rational Compassion*. New York: Ecco, 2016.

Boggs, Abigail, Eli Meyerhoff, Nick Mitchell, and Zach Schwartz-Weinstein. "Abolitionist University Studies: An Invitation." *Abolition*, August 2019.

Boym, Svetlana. *The Future of Nostalgia*. New York: Basic Books, 2001.

Briggs, Vernon M., Jr. *Mexican Migration and the U.S. Labor Market: A Mounting Issue for the Seventies*. Center for the Study of Human Resources and the Bureau of Business Research. Austin: University of Texas Press, 1975.

Brown, Elspeth H., and Thy Phu, eds. *Feeling Photography*. Durham, NC: Duke University Press, 2014.

Byrd, Jodi A. *The Transit of Empire: Indigenous Critiques of Colonialism*. Minneapolis: University of Minnesota Press, 2011.

Cadava, Eduardo, and Paola Cortés-Rocca. "Notes on Love and Photography." *October* 116 (2006): 3–34.

Chicago Department of Development. *Historic City: The Settlement of Chicago*. Chicago: City of Chicago, Department of Development and Planning, 1976.

Combahee River Collective. "The Combahee River Collective Statement." In *How We Get Free: Black Feminism and the Combahee River Collective*, edited by Keeanga-Yamahtta Taylor, 15–27. Chicago: Haymarket Books, 2012.

Cotera, María Eugenia. "El Museo del Norte: Passionate Praxis on the Streets of Detroit." In *The Latina/o Midwest Reader*, edited by Omar Valerio-Jiménez, Santiago Vaquera-Vásquez, and Claire F. Fox, 197–210. Champaign: University of Illinois Press, 2017.

Darwin, Charles. *The Expression of the Emotions in Man and Animals*. 1872. New York: Penguin Classics, 2009.

De Genova, Nicholas. *Working the Boundaries: Race, Space, and "Illegality" in Mexican Chicago*. Durham, NC: Duke University Press, 2005.

Doane, Mary Ann. *The Emergence of Cinematic Time: Modernity, Contingency, the Archive*. Cambridge, MA: Harvard University Press, 2002.

Duncan, Edgar H. "The Literature of Alchemy and Chaucer's Canon's Yeoman's Tale: Framework, Theme, and Characters." *Speculum* 43, no. 4 (1968): 633–56.

Edwards, Elizabeth. "Objects of Affect: Photography beyond the Image." *Annual Review of Anthropology* 41 (2012): 221–34.

Espinosa, Gastón, and Mario T. García, eds. *Mexican American Religions: Spirituality, Activism, and Culture*. Durham, NC: Duke University Press, 2008.

Figueroa-Vásquez, Yomaira. *Decolonizing Diasporas: Radical Mappings of Afro-Atlantic Literature*. Evanston, IL: Northwestern University Press, 2020.

Flores, John H., Frances R. Aparício, Juan Mora-Torres, and María de los Angeles Torres, eds. *The Mexican Revolution in Chicago: Immigration Politics from the Early Twentieth Century to the Cold War*. Champaign: University of Illinois Press, 2018.

Florestal, Marjorie. "Is a Burrito a Sandwich? Exploring Race, Class, and Culture in Contracts." *Michigan Journal of Race and Law* 14, no. 1 (2008): 1–59.

Gaskill, Nicholas. *Chromographia: American Literature and the Modernization of Color.* Minneapolis: University of Minnesota Press, 2018.

Ginzburg, Carlo. *Myths, Emblems, Clues.* Translated by John Tedeschi and Anne C. Tedeschi. London: Hutchinson Radius, 1990.

Goffe, Tao Leigh. "Sugarwork: The Gastropoetics of Afro-Asia after the Plantation." *Asian Diasporic Visual Cultures and the Americas* 5, nos. 1–2 (2019): 31–56.

Gómez, Laura E. *Manifest Destinies: The Making of the Mexican American Race.* New York: New York University Press, 2007.

Gómez-Quiñones, Juan. *Chicano Politics: Reality and Promise, 1940–1990.* Albuquerque: University of New Mexico Press, 1990.

Goodman, Kevis. "'Uncertain Disease': Nostalgia, Pathologies of Motion, Practices of Reading." *Studies in Romanticism* 49, no. 2 (2010): 197–227.

Goodrich, Peter. *Law in the Courts of Love: Literature and Other Minor Jurisprudences.* New York: Routledge, 2013.

Grosz, Elizabeth. *Becoming Undone: Darwinian Reflections on Life, Politics, and Art.* Durham, NC: Duke University Press, 2011.

Gumbs, Alexis Pauline. *Dub: Finding Ceremony.* Durham, NC: Duke University Press, 2020.

Gumbs, Alexis Pauline. *M Archive: After the End of the World.* Durham, NC: Duke University Press, 2018.

Gumbs, Alexis Pauline. *Spill: Scenes of Black Feminist Fugitivity.* Durham, NC: Duke University Press, 2016.

Gumbs, Alexis. "That Transformative Dark Thing." *New Inquiry*, May 19, 2015.

Gutiérrez, José Angel. *The Making of a Chicano Militant: Lessons from Cristal.* Madison: University of Wisconsin Press, 1998.

Hartman, Saidiya. *Lose Your Mother: A Journey along the Atlantic Slave Route.* New York: Farrar, Straus and Giroux, 2006.

Holland, Sharon. "When Characters Lack Character: A Biomythography." *PMLA* 123, no. 5 (2008): 1494–1502.

Holmes, Oliver Wendell. "The Stereoscope and the Stereograph." *Atlantic Monthly*, June 1859.

hooks, bell. *All about Love: New Visions.* New York: Harper, 2000.

Huerta, Monica. "The Burrito Dream: Authenticity and Cultural Hybridity in Mexican Restaurants in Late-Twentieth-Century Chicago." AB honors thesis, Harvard University, 2003.

Huerta, Monica. "What's Mine: Involuntary Expressions, Modern Personality, and the Right to Privacy." *J19: The Journal of Nineteenth-Century Americanists* 4, no. 2 (2016): 359–89.

Jones-Correa, Michael. *Between Two Nations: The Political Predicament of Latinos in New York City.* Ithaca, NY: Cornell University Press, 1998.

Kelly, Michael J., and David Satola. "The Right to Be Forgotten." *University of Illinois Law Review* 1 (2017): 1–64.

Khanna, Neetu. *The Visceral Logics of Decolonization*. Durham, NC: Duke University Press, 2020.

Lew-Williams, Beth. *The Chinese Must Go: Violence, Exclusion, and the Making of the Alien in America*. Cambridge, MA: Harvard University Press, 2018.

Lindberg, Richard. *Passport's Guide to Ethnic Chicago: A Complete Guide to the Many Faces and Cultures of Chicago*. Lincolnwood, IL: Passport Books, 1993.

Locke, Richard Adams. *The Moon Hoax: Or, A Discovery That the Moon Has a Vast Population of Human Beings*. Boston: Gregg Press, 1975.

López, Ian Haney. *White by Law: The Legal Construction of Race*. New York: New York University Press, 1996.

"Los Mexicanos en Chicago." Chicago: Consulado General de México en Chicago, 1996.

Lozano, Rosina. *An American Language: The History of Spanish in the United States*. Berkeley: University of California Press, 2018.

Machado, Antonio. "Juan de Mairena—Sentencias, donaires, apuntes y recuerdos de un profesor apórifo." In *Prosas completas (1936–39)*, vol. 4 of *Poesía y prosa*, edited by O. Macrì, 1917. Madrid: Espasa-Calpe, 1989.

Marroquin, Nicole. "Youth as Engaged Cultural Workers: Benito Juárez High School and the Legacy of Student Uprisings on the Lower West Side of Chicago." *Visual Arts Research* 44, no. 2 (2018): 43–52.

Mensel, Robert E. "'Kodakers Lying in Wait': Amateur Photography and the Right of Privacy in New York, 1885–1915." *American Quarterly* 43, no. 1 (1991): 24–45.

Meyerhoff, Eli. *Beyond Education: Radical Studying for Another World*. Minneapolis: University of Minnesota Press, 2019.

Mitchell, Nick. "(Critical Ethnic Studies) Intellectual." *Critical Ethnic Studies* 1, no. 1 (2015): 86–94.

Mitchell, Nick. "Summertime Selves (On Professionalization)." *New Inquiry*, October 4, 2019.

Molina, Natalia. *How Race Is Made in America: Immigration, Citizenship, and the Historical Power of Racial Scripts*. Berkeley: University of California Press, 2014.

Moten, Fred. "Poetics of Violence." Lecture, Princeton University, Princeton, NJ, February 2019.

Muñoz, Carlos, Jr. *Youth, Identity, Power: The Chicano Movement*. New York: Verso, 1989.

Ngai, Mae M. "A Nation of Immigrants: A Short History of an Idea." Lecture, Princeton University, Princeton, NJ, October, 15, 2018.

Ngai, Sianne. "Theory of the Gimmick." *Critical Inquiry* 43, no. 2 (2017): 466–505.

Ngai, Sianne. *Ugly Feelings*. Cambridge, MA: Harvard University Press, 2005.

Ohmstede, Antonio Escobar, ed. *Los pueblos indios en los tiempos de Benito Juarez (1847–1872)*. Oaxaca, Mexico: Universidad Autónoma Benito Juárez, 2007.

Parisi, David, Mark Paterson, and Jason Edward Archer. "Haptic Media Studies." *New Media and Society* 19, no. 10 (2017): 1513–22.

Park, K-Sue. "Money, Mortgages, and the Conquest of America." *Law and Social Inquiry* 41, no. 4 (2016): 1006–35.

Phelan, Peggy. *Unmarked: The Politics of Performance.* New York: Routledge, 1993.

Pinderhughes, Dianne M. *Race and Ethnicity in Chicago Politics: A Reexamination of Pluralist Theory.* Champaign: University of Illinois Press, 1987.

Prescod-Weinstein, Chanda. *The Disordered Cosmos: A Journey into Dark Matter, Spacetime, and Dreams Deferred.* New York: Bold Type Books, 2021. Prodger, Phillip. *Darwin's Camera: Art and Photography in the Theory of Evolution.* Oxford: Oxford University Press, 2009.

Robinson, Cedric. *Black Marxism: The Making of the Black Radical Tradition.* Chapel Hill: University of North Carolina Press, 1983.

Rosales, Steven. "Fighting the Peace at Home: Mexican American Veterans and the 1944 GI Bill of Rights." *Pacific Historical Review* 80, no. 4 (2011): 597–627.

Sánchez, George J. *Becoming Mexican American: Ethnicity, Culture and Identity in Chicano Los Angeles, 1900–1945.* Oxford: Oxford University Press, 1995.

Sedgwick, Eve Kosofsky. *Touching Feeling: Affect, Pedagogy, Performativity.* Durham, NC: Duke University Press, 2003.

Seremetakis, C. Nadia. *Sensing the Everyday: Dialogues from Austerity Greece.* New York: Routledge, 2019.

Serpell, Namwali. "The Banality of Empathy." *New York Review of Books,* March 3, 2019.

Sharpe, Christina. *In the Wake: On Blackness and Being.* Durham, NC: Duke University Press, 2016.

Shirazi, Ava. "The Mirror and the Senses: Materiality and Aesthetics in the Ancient Greek World." Unpublished manuscript, 2019.

Steedman, Carolyn. *Dust: The Archives and Cultural History.* New Brunswick, NJ: Rutgers University Press, 2002.

Stewart, Kathleen. *Ordinary Affects.* Durham, NC: Duke University Press, 2007.

Stewart, Susan. *Cinder.* Minneapolis: Graywolf Press, 2017.

Tompkins, Kyla Wazana. *Racial Indigestion: Eating Bodies in the 19th Century.* New York: New York University Press, 2012.

Tuck, Eve, and K. Wayne Yang. "Decolonization Is Not a Metaphor." *Decolonization: Indigeneity, Education, and Society* 1, no. 1 (2012): 1–40.

Valerio-Jiménez, Omar, Santiago Vaquera-Vásquez, and Claire F. Fox. "Introduction: History, Placemaking, and Cultural Contributions." In *The Latina/o Midwest Reader,* edited by Omar Valerio-Jiménez, Santiago Vaquera-Vásquez, and Claire F. Fox, 1–22. Champaign: University of Illinois Press, 2017.

Valerio-Jiménez, Omar, Santiago Vaquera-Vásquez, and Claire F. Fox, eds. *The Latina/o Midwest Reader.* Champaign: University of Illinois Press, 2017.

Vida, István Kornél. "The 'Great Moon Hoax' of 1835." In "Lifelong Search for Meaning: Special Double Issue in Honor of Professor Donald E. Morse" (special issue), *Hungarian Journal of English and American Studies,* 18, nos. 1–2 (2012): 431–41.

Viego, Antonio. *Dead Subjects: Toward a Politics of Loss in Latino Studies.* Durham, NC: Duke University Press, 2007.

Young, Julia G. "Cristero Diaspora: Mexican Immigrants, the U.S. Catholic Church, and Mexico's Cristero War, 1926–29." *Catholic Historical Review* 98, no. 2 (2012): 271–300.

Young, Julia G. *Mexican Exodus: Emigrants, Exiles, and Refugees of the Cristero War.* New York: Oxford University Press, 2015.

CPSIA information can be obtained
at www.ICGtesting.com
Printed in the USA
LVHW082129120821
695175LV00012B/398